2-

Happy Birthday to a   11/28/01
delicious friend!
Love,
Judi

# Two for Tonight

Love begins in the kitchen!

Jacques E. Haeringer

# Two for Tonight

*Pure Romance from L'Auberge Chez François*

## JACQUES E. HAERINGER

**Bartleby Press**

SILVER SPRING, MARYLAND

*Front dust jacket photograph:*
*Fillets of Sole with Oysters and Alsatian Crémant Sauce (page 155)*

Text design and layout by Ross Feldner
Illustrations by Laura-Leigh Palmer
Photography by Dean Ray

Manufactured in the United States

PUBLISHED BY

**Bartleby Press**

11141 GEORGIA AVENUE
SILVER SPRING, MARYLAND 20902

Library of Congress Cataloging-in-Publication Data

Haeringer, Jacques E.
        Two for tonight: pure romance from L'Auberge Chez François /
Jacques E. Haeringer.
            p. cm.
        Includes index.
        ISBN 0-910155-43-7
        1. Cookery, French 2. L'Auberge Chez François (Great Falls, Va.) I. Title
TX719.H262    2001
641.5944—dc21                                            00-065193

*For Evelyn*
*In Loving Memory*

# Acknowledgements

First, my appreciation goes to my father, François. *Merci beaucoup*, Papa for teaching me how to cook.

*Two for Tonight* would not have been possible without the assistance of my mother, Marie-Antionette, and my brothers, Robert and Paul. In addition, my son Marc provided important research and my daughter Madeleine made many helpful suggestions.

Hats off to the multi-talented Rita Calvert, food stylist for the photographs in the book. Her research was very beneficial, and her culinary flair, and all-around good cheer were invaluable.

Charles Bonfield prepared the dishes for the book photographs as well as recipe testing and suggestions. Judith Hartman of Plate du Jour and Jean-Philip of Kruko, Inc. generously provided plates and linens.

I am grateful to Dr. Nicholas J. Gonzalez for generously sharing his vast knowledge of nutrition.

Special recognition goes to the following recipe testers and tasters: Chef Chun Ik Oh, Pastry Chef William Sobalvarro, Robert Betman, Salvador Benitez, Don Carson, Brian Murphy, William Walden, and the entire kitchen staff at L'Auberge Chez François. The dining room staff also performed above and beyond the call of duty.

Paula Leckey and Rona Herdman helped with editing, proof reading, and generally kept me organized, a formidable task indeed. My cousin, Christian Bisch in Alsace, shared many of her recipe ideas.

This book project would not have come together without the efforts of my friend, publisher *extraordinaire*, Jeremy Kay.

A romantic occasion requires two. Every dish I prepare for Carol Huebner is cause for celebration. Thanks for your love, inspiration, and for being *my* special someone.

# Contents

# Introduction

Roses smell fine.
Candy tastes sweet,
but a romantic repast
is a much better treat.

Romantic celebrations are a tradition at L'Auberge Chez François. You might even say special events like engagements, weddings, and anniversaries are our *raison d'être*. It is a tradition based on our philosophy that life's memorable moments are not complete without a festive meal. The pleasures of the table, fine food and wine, are an essential part of a passionate life. Good food whets the appetite, which in turn stimulates the entire person, promoting a well-being and excitement that leads to love. Yes, we are most susceptible to love after a festive and nutritious meal. Couples return to our restaurant year after year to renew and reaffirm the romance in their lives. We supply the food, ambience, and service; they bring their own romantic magic.

At home, preparing a repast for your someone special is an act of love, much more significant than presenting candy or flowers. The food is tempting, but it is the energy you put into the preparation and serving of the meal that is sexy.

Rather than prepare everything ahead, which is not always practical, put the finishing touches together right before your special someone's eyes; this will therefore more closely resemble the way meals are prepared in fine restaurants. Items such as stocks and garnishes are prepared in advance, but the main ingredient is cooked and the sauce finished at the last moment, just before serving. Bring that special someone into the kitchen first—who knows what may follow. Love begins in the kitchen.

## TO YOUR HEALTH

If you prepare a romantic meal for your special someone, make it as wholesome and nourishing as possible. The vitality and stamina necessary to love and respond to being loved requires robust, good health that comes mainly from proper food choices. The use of whole pure ingredients will result in a better tasting and more nutritious repast. Knowing that you are using the best ingredients is important and lends to the romantic mood.

I try to use organically grown produce as well as organic sources of meat and poultry. Organic fruits, grains, nuts, seeds, and vegetables are grown without synthetic fertilizers, chemicals, or pesticides. Organic free-range cattle and poultry are raised without the use of hormones, antibiotics, and synthetic growth stimulants. These products are increasingly available to those knowledgeable consumers who seek them out. Most areas have a health food store or co-op.

Many chefs also try to utilize organic products because they are often the highest quality and most nutritious. Those of us in the kitchen are responding to the genuine concerns of our patrons. Chef's organizations, such as Chef's Collaborative, promote the use of organic products and have set up a resource network for these products.

Try to obtain as many whole, pure ingredients as possible, but do not hesitate to make a recipe merely because one or two of the ingredients are not organic. It is not what you eat occasionally that determines your level of health but your diet in general. When you have the choice follow the suggestions; if not, remember that if you worry about every bite and every sip, stress will kill you long before cholesterol.

Here are guidelines I use when preparing a romantic menu:

Using pure water for cooking will improve the taste. The chlorine and other chemicals found in our drinking water tend to alter taste. Brew a pot of coffee or tea using bottled water, then do the same with tap water. Taste the difference! At home, I personally use a reverse osmosis filter to obtain pure water for drinking and cooking.

The best way to cook vegetables is to steam them, thereby preserving most of the nutritional content. Boiling a vegetable leeches valuable nutrients and deposits them into the water; those nutrients are lost if the liquid is thrown out. As often as possible, cooking liquids are incorporated into the recipes to retain nutrients.

In general, use whole grains and flours. There are notable exceptions, such as dusting before sautéing or making a pie crust (whole wheat just does not work as well). Refined grain products such as white flour and white rice have been stripped of their nutrients. During the refining process, 22 essential nutrients, including fiber are removed. So-called enriched products have three to four nutrients replaced, but remain nutritionally inferior.

Salt is one of the oldest commodities traded by man. For most of us, salting to taste is not a problem. However, use natural sea or mineral salt as it is unprocessed, and therefore contains important minerals and trace elements.

I recommend the use of evaporated cane juice instead of white sugar. Evaporated cane juice is the whole dried sap of the sugar cane and contains many nutrients lost in regular sugar. This product is now more readily available and is used one-for-one in place of white sugar. Evaporated cane juice adds little favor. Other sweeteners, such as honey or maple syrup, are also recommended. You should keep in mind that sugar adds only sweetness. Honey or maple syrup will impart distinctive flavors often enhancing but decidedly altering the finished product.

I recommend using extra virgin olive oil or other cold processed oils as they retain essential nutrients lost during the heat associated with refining.

A certain amount of raw or lightly-cooked food in the diet is essential to good health. We are the only species on the planet that eats our food cooked. Uncooked foods such as raw fruits, vegetables, juices and salad along with sprouted grains and sprouted beans contain enzymes and nutrients that are healthy for you. These nutrients are "heat sensitive" and are destroyed easily. Don't forget to enjoy raw oysters and Steak Tartare as they, too, provide essential nutrients. Dine in almost any Paris bistro and you will see many platters of raw oysters and Steak Tartare everywhere. Perhaps this is part of the French paradox, the lower incidence of heart disease despite the relatively high-fat diet.

Despite all the warnings of past decades, we have now returned to our senses and realize that, for most of us, red meat is an essential component of our diets. After all, we did not claw our way to the top of the food chain to eat only vegetables. Game should be considered health food because wild game forages for its natural diet. We have eaten game for millions of years and our systems are geared to the leaner game rather than the fatty domesticated animals.

Stocks and sauces made from the slow reduction of meat, vegetable, and fish are some of the most nutritious delights on the planet and are found in most cultures. The gelatin found in the stocks aids digestion and protein utilization. Freshly made stock, especially fish, is rich in trace minerals and iodine, often absent in land-based foods. Besides the health benefits, stocks are the basis for delicious and satisfying sauces. The extra flavors from the creation of a well-prepared sauce heightens the overall satisfaction of any enticing dish.

If you go to the extra effort to prepare your own stocks and sauces it will be most appreciated. The final product will be both nutritious and delicious. Preparing good stocks and sauces at home is not technically difficult as most of the preparation time is unsupervised simmering. However, the overall time factor will certainly give some pause. To save time, I suggest making a fairly large quantity of stock and freezing portions in small containers for later use.

You will find a number of sauces based in cream or butter in the book. Though the health merits of cream and butter-based sauces will endlessly be debated, they are fine in moderation and are very fast and easy to prepare at home, allowing the chef to create any number of flavors. A couple of tablespoons of sauce is all that is required. Go ahead—enjoy yourself.

Many upscale food stores sell in-house prepared stocks and sauces. Your favorite restaurant might be persuaded to sell you a quantity. There are good sauce bases available that are easy to use, give quite satisfactory results, and are free of objectionable ingredients.

Try to cook according to the guidelines and you will have the strength and good health to be a little naughty now and then.

I have written these recipes using ingredients that will make them as nutritious as possible. Do the best you can, but do not allow any of the guidelines to dampen the pure pleasure of preparing a romantic meal for the one you love.

## HOW TO USE THIS BOOK

The recipes are divided into six thematic chapters, each setting a tone for a certain time of day or romantic scenario. "Breakfast in Bed" and "After Midnight" contain recipes for small plates and desserts. The remaining thematic chapters contain appetizers, main courses, and desserts. The thematic groupings are merely suggestions as the recipes are easily adapted to more than one situation. I have also included suggested menus for each chapter. The last chapter covers basic recipes.

Unless otherwise noted all recipes serve two. You will find many recipes in the Basics chapter that are for larger quantities as it is impractical to make very small amounts of such items as stocks. Make these types of recipes in larger quantities and then freeze the unused quantities for use later. Then have some fun and cook to your heart's content.

Please see *www.chefjacques.com* for ingredient source information.

# Breakfast in Bed

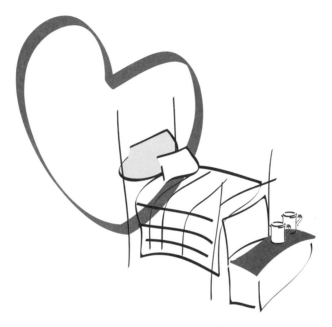

Sunday, mid-morning. It was a wonderful, romantic evening and now you gently nudge your sweetheart, who wakes to see your seductive smile and a tray with a split of Champagne and assorted goodies. Voilà. Your culinary talents will set the tone for an entire day of pleasure and keep the magic going a while longer.

Breakfast in Bed features small plates including recipes such as Smoked Fish Benedict, my seafood version of the classic. The recipes may be partially prepared in advance to minimize time in the kitchen. Prepare one or more for your special someone depending on your mood. Your thoughtfulness will surely be rewarded.

# Suggested Menus

◆◆◆

Smoked Fish Benedict
Warm Roquefort Tart

Soft Boiled Eggs with Salmon Roe
Cinnamon Trout
Exotic Fruit Salad

Scrambled Eggs with Caviar
Apple Napoleon

Cheese Soufflé
Pear Crêpes

Pipérade
Fruit Crumble

# Smoked Fish Benedict

*After years of disfavor, eggs are now recognized as one of the most nourishing foods on earth. In ancient Rome, preparing eggs for one's lover was thought to be a sign of deep affection. This is a seafood variation of the classic eggs benedict.*

THE POTATO AND APPLE PANCAKE:

> 1 large Russet potato (10 ounces)
> 1 Granny Smith apple
> Sea salt
> Freshly ground pepper
> Pinch of cinnamon
> 4 tablespoons butter

THE FISH BENEDICT:

> 2 large organic eggs
> Sea salt
> Freshly ground pepper
> 4 ounces assorted smoked seafood: scallops, mussels, shrimp, salmon or tuna
> $^1/_2$ ounce Osetra caviar
> 4 tablespoons Hollandaise Sauce (page 242)

## TO PREPARE THE PANCAKES:

*Preheat the oven to 375 degrees.*

Peel and core the apple. Quarter the apple and cut each quarter into 4 slices.

Peel, wash, and shred the potato. Place the shredded potato in a small bowl and season with salt, pepper, and cinnamon.

Heat 2 tablespoons of butter in small sauté pan or 5-6 inch diameter crêpe pan. When the butter begins to brown, place $^1/_2$ of the apple slices in a circle in the pan and cover with $^1/_2$ of the prepared potato to form a pancake. Sauté over high heat for approximately 2 minutes until golden brown, turn over and place the pan in a preheated 375 degree oven for about 8-10 minutes, until the potato is cooked through. Remove from the oven and keep warm.

Repeat to make second pancake.

Serve with the apple side up.

*Hint:* Pancakes may be prepared ahead and reheated before serving.

## TO ASSEMBLE THE DISH:

Poach the 2 eggs.

Warm the 2 pancakes and assorted smoked seafood (scallops, mussels, etc.) in a 350 degree oven for 2-3 minutes.

Place 1 potato and apple pancake on each of two warm plates.

Place a slice of the smoked salmon in the center of each pancake.

Place a poached egg on the smoked salmon.

Arrange the remaining warm smoked seafood around the pancake.

Coat each poached egg with about 2 tablespoons of Hollandaise Sauce and top with caviar.

Serve immediately.

*Hint:* Use Russet or Idaho potatoes for this recipe. The low moisture and high starch content helps hold the pancake together.

# Scrambled Eggs with Caviar

*I personally serve Osetra caviar from the Caspian Sea to my special someone. The Osetra eggs are grayish brown, often with a golden tint, and have a superior flavor.*

>   2 jumbo organic eggs
>   1 ounce Osetra caviar
>   1 rounded teaspoon butter
>   1 teaspoon of heavy whipping cream or crème fraîche
>   Sea salt
>   Freshly ground pepper
>   Country bread

Carefully cut off the top $\frac{1}{3}$ (narrow end) of the eggs with a serrated edged knife or kitchen shears with the goal of reusing the egg shell.

Pour out the eggs into a bowl. Add the heavy cream, whisking thoroughly. Season with salt and pepper.

Heat the butter in a small sauté pan. When the butter begins to foam, add the egg mixture and scramble until just set. Remove pan from heat and mix in $\frac{1}{2}$ of the caviar.

Fill the 2 egg shells with the scrambled eggs and top each with $\frac{1}{2}$ of the remaining caviar.

Serve immediately with buttered toast points.

*Hint:* It may not be necessary to season the eggs with salt, as the caviar is salty.

*Variation:* Scramble the eggs with 1 teaspoon of chopped truffle. Top with chopped truffle.

# Truffle Omelet

*Gourmands have considered truffles aphrodisiacs since ancient times. Truffles, which cannot be cultivated, are expensive because they are hunted and unearthed by pigs or dogs. A little goes a long way however, and the exotic aroma and flavor are sure to excite the senses.*

> 4 jumbo organic eggs
> 1 ounce of fresh black truffles
> 1 teaspoon olive oil
> 1 tablespoon butter
> Sea salt
> Freshly ground pepper

## PREPARE THE NIGHT BEFORE SERVING:

Place whole eggs and truffles in a bowl. Cover tightly with plastic wrap and set in refrigerator overnight. The eggs will absorb the truffle fragrance.

## TO PREPARE THE OMELET:

Brush the truffle to remove any dirt. With a sharp knife, cut a truffle in two and cut 4 very thin slices to be used as garnish. Coarsely chop the remaining truffles.

Break the eggs into a medium bowl, season with salt and pepper, and whisk thoroughly. Stir in the chopped truffle.

Place a well-seasoned omelet pan over high heat and add the oil and butter. Just as the butter begins to brown, pour the prepared eggs into the pan. Shake the pan in a back and forth motion and stir the eggs with a fork or spatula until the desired doneness. Fold cooked eggs over to form the omelet and turn out into a large warm serving platter.

Top the omelet with the 4 reserved truffle slices.

Serve with country bread.

# Soft Boiled Eggs with Salmon Roe

*Eggs are packed with vital nutrients that will undoubtedly boost your stamina. This combination of eggs and caviar surely would have been enjoyed by the likes of Casanova.*

> 2 jumbo organic eggs
> Sea salt
> Freshly ground pepper
> $1/2$ ounce salmon caviar

Bring a small pot of water to a boil. Carefully slide the eggs into the boiling water with the aid of a slotted spoon.

Set the timer for 3 minutes and lower heat to a gentle boil.

Remove eggs from the water with the slotted spoon and place each in an egg cup, large end up.

Carefully cut off the top $1/3$ of the egg shell with a serrated edged knife.

Lightly salt and pepper the exposed egg and top each with $1/2$ of the salmon caviar.

Serve immediately with toasted country bread.

*Variation:* Use black caviar.

# Cheese Soufflés

*I should not let this secret get out but chefs are now adding a little Viagra to their soufflés (just kidding). This new formulation has greater staying power and heightened presentation.*

> 4 tablespoons lightly salted butter
> 6 tablespoons flour
> 1½ cups milk
> ½ teaspoon sea salt
> Pinch of freshly ground pepper
> Pinch of nutmeg
> 8 tablespoons (3 ounces) grated cheese: Parmesan, Gruyère, etc.
> 3-4 additional tablespoons of the grated cheese
> 4 egg yolks
> 4 egg whites

Melt 2 tablespoons of the butter in a heavy saucepan over moderate heat. Add the flour, salt, pepper, and nutmeg and mix thoroughly. Slowly, pour the milk over the roux, whisking constantly. Bring to a boil, continue whisking, and allow to bubble for 2 minutes. Whisk thoroughly, as the mixture will scorch easily. Remove saucepan from heat and scrape the contents into a medium mixing bowl.

*Preheat the oven to 375 degrees.*

Allow to cool for 2-3 minutes.

Add the 8 tablespoons of grated cheese to the mixture and blend thoroughly.

Whisk in the egg yolks two by two.

Completely coat the insides of two 12-ounce soufflé dishes with the remaining 2 tablespoons of butter and "flour" with the additional grated cheese.

Whip the egg whites until they form soft peaks and gently fold into the egg and cheese mixture.

Fill the prepared soufflé molds to the top with the mixture and bake in a preheated 375 degree oven for about 20 minutes until well risen and golden brown. Serve immediately.

# Pipérade

*This dish is a Basque specialty consisting of a rich stew of tomatoes and peppers, seasoned with onion and garlic, cooked in olive oil or goose fat, then mixed with beaten eggs and lightly scrambled.*

> 2 tablespoons olive oil or rendered duck fat
> 1/3 cup finely chopped onions
> 1 large ripe tomato (1/2 cup)
> 1 bell pepper, cored, seeded, and small diced, (1/2 cup)
> 1/2 teaspoon finely chopped garlic
> 1 teaspoon tomato paste
> Pinch of fresh chopped thyme or *Herbs de Provence*
> Sea salt
> Freshly ground pepper
> Pinch of cayenne pepper or *Piment D'Espelette*
> 3 large eggs
> 2 slices of *Jambon de Bayonne* (thinly sliced)

Bring 1 quart of water to a boil and add the tomato for 10 to 20 seconds. Lift the tomato out of the water with a slotted spoon and drop into a bowl of cold water. Cool the tomato a few moments and remove from the water. Peel off the skin and cut out the stem. Slice the tomato in half and place in a large-holed colander set over a bowl. Press the tomato halves to force out the juice and seeds. Coarsely chop the tomato pulp and set aside.

Heat the olive oil in a large casserole over medium heat. Add the chopped onions, tomato, diced pepper, garlic, tomato paste, and thyme; simmer for approximately 15 minutes until the vegetables are tender and the sauce has thickened. Season with salt, pepper, and cayenne.

While the sauce cooks, sauté the ham slices in oil or rendered fat.

Beat the eggs with a wire whisk. Slowly pour the beaten eggs into the hot sauce, stirring constantly with a large kitchen spoon. Cook until the eggs are just set and creamy.

Place a slice of ham on a warm plate and top with the mixture. Serve at once with slices of toasted country bread.

*Variation:* Substitute country ham for the *Jambon de Bayonne.*

Pipérade may also be served with ham on the side.

*Piment D'Espelette* are peppers from the Basque country. They are sometimes found dried and ground in specialty food stores.

# Cinnamon Trout

*This dish, with its unusual combination of flavors, will spice up any cozy brunch.*

THE HERB BUTTER:

    2 tablespoons butter
    1 tablespoon chopped fresh tarragon
    $\frac{1}{2}$ teaspoon ground cinnamon
    Sea salt
    Freshly ground pepper

THE TROUT:

    2 3-4 ounce skinless trout fillets
    1 teaspoon oil
    $\frac{1}{2}$ tablespoon butter
    $\frac{1}{2}$ cup flour
    $\frac{1}{2}$ teaspoon ground cinnamon
    1 teaspoon capers
    1 tablespoon raw pumpkin seeds

## TO PREPARE THE BUTTER:

Soften the butter and place in a small bowl.

Add the chopped tarragon, $\frac{1}{2}$ of the ground cinnamon, and a pinch of salt and pepper. Mix thoroughly. Taste and adjust seasonings. Set aside. The herb butter may be prepared a day ahead.

## TO PREPARE THE TROUT:

Lightly salt and pepper the trout fillets and dredge in the flour.

Place the oil and $\frac{1}{2}$ tablespoon of butter in a medium sauté pan large enough to hold the trout fillets, over medium heat.

When the butter begins to foam, sauté the trout fillets, approximately $1\frac{1}{2}$ minutes per side, until just cooked through. Transfer the cooked fillets to a serving platter with the aid of a slotted spatula. Dust the cooked fillets with $\frac{1}{2}$ teaspoon of cinnamon.

Scatter the well-drained capers and pumpkin seeds around the platter.

Divide the seasoned butter between the 2 fillets and place platter under a preheated broiler to slightly melt.

Serve with boiled potatoes.

*Variation:* Use sliced almonds rather than the pumpkin seeds.

# Warm Roquefort Tart

*This delectable combination of flavors and textures is sure to do the trick! Not just for dessert, try this tart in place of a cheese course.*

> 1 Golden or Red Delicious apple
> 2 tablespoons butter
> 2 tablespoons evaporated cane juice or sugar
> 4 tablespoons Roquefort cheese
> 2 4-5 inch circles Puff Pastry (page 248)

Sandwich the 2 circles of puff pastry dough between 2 baking sheets. Bake at 350 degrees for 8-10 minutes. Remove the top sheet pan and allow the dough to brown. Remove from oven and allow to cool on the sheet pan.

Peel, core, and quarter the apple. Cut each quarter in half. Place a small sauté pan over high heat and sprinkle the sugar in the pan. When the sugar begins to caramelize, add the butter and the apple wedges and toss to coat with the sugar. Cook for approximately 2 minutes until wedges are al dente and slightly caramelized. Transfer to a dish to cool.

## TO PREPARE THE TART:

Place 4 of the apple wedges around each of the pre-cooked disks of dough in a spiral. Crumble the Roquefort cheese and top each tart with half. This may be prepared several hours ahead and refrigerated.

## TO SERVE:

Heat the tarts in a *425 degree oven* for 4-5 minutes to thoroughly heat the cheese and apples. Do not completely melt the cheese. Transfer to warm plates.

*Variation:* Try using the Savory Pie Crust (page 248) rather than the Puff Pastry. Slices of country or sourdough bread may also be substituted for the pastry dough.

# Potato Rosti with Currant-Glazed Peaches

*Oprah Winfrey said, "My idea of heaven is a great big baked potato and someone to share it with." The fruit and potato combination may be served alone or makes an exciting garnish for pork or chicken dishes.*

THE POTATO CAKE:

> 1 pound large Yukon gold potatoes, peeled
> 2 tablespoons clarified butter

THE GLAZED PEACHES:

> $\frac{1}{2}$ cup currant jelly
> 3 tablespoons balsamic vinegar
> 2 peaches, peeled, pitted, and cut into eighths lengthwise

Fit the work bowl of a food processor with the julienne blade. Cut the potatoes to fit the feed tube and process the potatoes into julienne strips, or cut the potatoes by hand into very thin match sticks (makes about 3 cups). Rinse the potatoes in several changes of water; drain. Spread potatoes out on a kitchen towel to dry. Roll the towel and potatoes up and squeeze tightly to extrude all excess water. Potatoes will begin to darken within $\frac{1}{2}$ hour.

In a 14-inch non-stick skillet, melt butter. When the butter just begins to brown, add potatoes and spread evenly. Press down lightly. Turn heat to low and cook for 10-15 minutes until lightly golden. Flip cake over by turning onto a separate plate and then sliding back into the same skillet. Brown bottom side for another 10 minutes. When browned, slide onto heat-proof platter. May be kept warm in a low oven.

## WHILE POTATOES COOK:

In a medium skillet, melt jelly and balsamic vinegar. When melted, add peach wedges and simmer until tender, about 8 minutes. Place in serving bowl and keep warm.

Arrange the peach wedges around the crispy potato cake and spoon any jelly remaining in the pan over the peach wedges.

Cut crispy potato cake into wedges and place on individual serving plates. May be topped with a dollop of crème fraîche or sour cream.

*Variation:* You may substitute other seasonal fruit, such as apples, plums, or berries.

# Avocado Crème Brûlée

*Avocado is actually a fruit that has been considered a sexual stimulant as far back as the ancient Aztecs. Avocados are rich in protein. This combination makes an unusual dessert.*

    1 large ripe avocado
    1 tablespoon apple cider vinegar

THE CUSTARD:

    $1/2$ cup heavy whipping cream
    2 tablespoons honey
    Pinch of sea salt
    Pinch of cayenne pepper
    2 large eggs
    $1/2$ teaspoon vanilla extract
    3-4 tablespoons evaporated cane juice or sugar

THE TOMATO CONFIT GARNISH:

    1 large ripe tomato
    2 tablespoons water
    $1^1/2$ tablespoons evaporated cane juice or lightly flavored honey
    1 tablespoon lemon juice
    Reserved tomato juice
    $1/2$ teaspoon vanilla extract

SPECIAL EQUIPMENT:

    2 1-cup size gratin dishes

## TO PREPARE THE AVOCADO:

Cut the avocado in half lengthwise. Carefully remove the pit and peel off the skin. Cut into $1/4$-inch lengthwise slices. Place the slices in a shallow bowl and coat with the vinegar to prevent discoloration.

Pour off the vinegar and divide the slices between the two gratin dishes, covering the bottoms.

## TO PREPARE THE CUSTARD:

Combine the cream, honey, salt, and cayenne pepper in a small saucepan and place over moderate flame. Heat until the mixture just begins to boil and remove from flame.

Beat the eggs in a medium glass or stainless steel bowl.

Slowly pour in the scalded cream, whisking constantly.

Add the vanilla extract.

*Preheat the oven to 275 degrees.*

Set the gratin dishes into a shallow baking dish or pan at least one inch deep. Fill the gratin dishes with the custard mix. Pour hot tap water into the baking dish to a level halfway up the sides of the gratin dishes.

Place the baking dish in the preheated oven and bake until the custard is set, about 35 minutes. Test for doneness by inserting a toothpick into the custard; custard is set if toothpick comes out clean. Refrigerate and allow to cool completely.

### TO PREPARE THE TOMATO CONFIT:
Bring a quart of water to a boil.

Add the tomato to the pot of boiling water for about 20 seconds. Lift the tomato out of the boiling water with a slotted spoon and drop into a bowl of cold water. Cool the tomato a few moments and remove from the cold water.

Peel off the skin and remove the stem. Slice the tomato in half and place in a colander set over a bowl. Press the tomato halves to force out the juice and seeds. Strain the juice to remove the seeds and reserve. Thinly slice the tomato halves and reserve while preparing the syrup.

### TO PREPARE THE SYRUP:
Combine the reserved tomato juice, water, honey, and lemon juice in a small heavy saucepan, bring to a boil over high heat and reduce to a thick syrup, about 4 minutes. Add the thinly sliced tomato and vanilla extract. Bring to a boil, reduce heat, and simmer for 5 minutes until the tomato slices are tender. Remove from heat and chill.

### TO FINISH THE CRÈME BRÛLÉE:
*Preheat the broiler.*

Thinly cover each dish with 1½-2 tablespoons of evaporated cane juice, sugar, or brown sugar. Raise the oven rack as high as possible and place the prepared custards under the broiler. Melt and lightly brown the sweetener, about 1 minute. Pay close attention, as the sweetener burns very quickly. Allow to cool and refrigerate.

Remove from refrigerator about ½ hour before serving as crème brûlée is best served at room temperature.

Garnish with 1 tablespoon of tomato confit.

*Hint:* To ensure getting a ripe avocado, plan to purchase it a few days ahead and let ripen to tenderness.

# Pear Crêpes

*The French poet Rabelais wrote,*
*"There is no match you might compare, To Master Cheese and Mistress Pear."*
*This presentation is simply marvelous.*

> ¹/₂ cup of raisins
> 2 tablespoons of Poire Williams or Cognac
> 2 ripe Bosch or Anjou pears
> 2 tablespoons butter
> ¹/₂ cup of maple syrup
> Pinch of cinnamon
> 4 tablespoons Roquefort cheese
> 4 crepes (page 251)

## TO PREPARE THE FILLING:

Place the raisins in a cup, add the cognac, and allow to macerate 1 hour.

Peel, quarter, and core the pears. Cut each quarter into 5-6 pieces. Melt the butter in a medium sauté pan. When the butter begins to brown, add the prepared pears, raisins, maple syrup, and cinnamon; lower heat and boil for about 5-7 minutes until pears are tender (cooking time will vary depending upon the ripeness of the pears). Taste and adjust seasonings; add more cognac, if desired, and keep warm.

## TO PREPARE THE CRÊPES:

Place the open crepes on a warm platter and divide the prepared pears among the 4 crepes. Place 1 tablespoon of the Roquefort cheese over the pears. Fold the crepes over, place in a 350 degree preheated oven for 3-4 minutes until warmed through. Serve immediately.

Garnish with a tablespoon of crème fraîche, if desired.

# Exotic Fruit Salad

*In Indian folklore, lovers' pledges made in the cooling shade of a mango tree would come to pass and eating a mango was thought to bring good fortune. Mangoes have hundreds of varieties and the best fruit is picked at dawn as the first rays of sun strike the tree, in the nude. Serving this exotic fruit salad always makes me want to run off to the islands with my special someone.*

> 1 mango
> 1 ripe papaya
> 1 peach or apple
> 1 kiwi
> ½ cup raspberries
> ½ cup sweet late harvest wine
> 1 lemon
> 2 tablespoons honey
> 12 mint leaves

Peel and cut the mango into thin slices.

Peel and cut the papaya into a large dice.

Cut the peach in half, remove pit and slice thinly.

Peel and slice kiwi into roundels

Place raspberries in a bowl with the other fruit.

Chop 10 mint leaves and add to the fruit.

Press the lemon to obtain the juice. Mix the lemon juice and honey together. Whisk the wine into the lemon and honey.

Pour the wine/honey syrup over the fruit and mix delicately.

Refrigerate for at least 2 hours.

Decorate with the remaining mint leaves before serving.

*Variation:* Use a late harvest Gewurstraminer or Sauternes.

# Fruit Crumble

*The only blue fruit, blueberries, contains a host of minerals such as iron and magnesium and is rich in Vitamins A and C. A crumble is a British dessert in which raw fruits are topped with a crumbly pastry mixture and baked.*

THE FRUIT:

>    8 ounces mixed berries: raspberries, strawberries,
>       blackberries, blueberries
>    1-2 tablespoons honey

THE TOPPING:

>    2 tablespoons unsalted butter
>    3 tablespoons all-purpose flour
>    3 tablespoons almond or hazelnut flour
>    2 tablespoons evaporated cane juice

## TO PREPARE THE FRUIT:

Remove any stems, clean the fruit, and place in the bottom of a shallow oven proof dish 6-8 inches in diameter. Depending on the ripeness of the fruit, drizzle 1-2 tablespoons of honey over the fruit.

## TO PREPARE THE TOPPING:

Cut the butter into small dice and allow to soften slightly. Place the flour, almond flour, and evaporated cane juice in a mixing bowl. Add the butter using the tips of your fingers. Mix to obtain a coarse meal.

## TO ASSEMBLE:

Cover the fruit with the coarse meal and place in a preheated 375 degree oven; bake until the crumble browns, approximately 12 minutes.

Serve warm with crème fraîche.

# Espresso Mousse

*Delight your special someone by serving this eye-opening mousse in espresso cups.*

  $^1/_2$ cup brewed espresso coffee
  1$^1/_2$ tablespoons honey
  $^1/_2$ teaspoon gelatin
  1 tablespoon water
  Pinch of salt
  1 cup of heavy whipping cream

Place the freshly-brewed espresso in a small saucepan, place over high heat, and reduce to $^1/_3$ cup to concentrate the flavor. Chill.

While the coffee is reducing, place the honey, gelatin, salt, and water in a small mixing bowl; allow the gelatin to soften for 5 minutes and set over a pot of boiling water. Heat for 1-2 minutes until the gelatin melts. Whisk thoroughly. Remove from heat and add the reduced espresso and mix completely.

Whip the heavy cream in a medium mixing bowl and chill.

Fold the espresso mixture into the heavy whipping cream with the aid of a rubber spatula.

Pipe or spoon the mousse into $^1/_2$-cup size or larger stem ware or dishes. Top the mousse with a pinch of cinnamon or cocoa powder, if desired.

*Hint:* Substitute 2 cups freshly brewed coffee, reduced to $^1/_3$ cup, if an espresso machine is unavailable. Decaffeinated coffee may also be substituted.

# Apple Napoleon

*Italian poet and libertine, Gabriele D'Annunzio, offered this method for evaluating a potential lover, "...I offer her an apple or pear to see how she eats it. Small mincing bites—the ladylike kind—they are not good. But if she crunches the fruit, salivates with pleasure, and crinkles her nose in enjoyment, this girl, my friend, should prove to be a redoubtable love partner." The "apple of your eye" will surely appreciate this dessert.*

THE NAPOLEON:

> 4 ounces Puff Pastry (page 248)
> 2 medium apples, Golden Delicious, Ginger Gold, Granny Smith
> 1 tablespoon butter
> 2 tablespoons evaporated cane juice or sugar
> 1 egg

THE CARAMEL SAUCE:

> 1½ tablespoons evaporated cane juice or sugar
> ⅓ cup heavy whipping cream

## TO PREPARE THE NAPOLEON:

Roll out the puff dough to a sheet 8 x 8 x ⅛-inch thick on a floured surface.

Cut 6 2½ x 4-inch rectangles of dough.

Place the puff pastry dough on a small sheet pan.

Allow the pastry dough to rest for 1 hour in the refrigerator.

*Preheat the oven to 375 degrees.*

Prick the dough using a fork and place another sheet pan on top to sandwich the dough.

Bake the puff pastry dough in a 350 degree oven for about 5 minutes. Remove the top sheet pan.

Thoroughly whisk the egg with 1 teaspoon of water.

Brush the puff pastry dough sections with the egg wash and lightly sprinkle with the evaporated cane juice. Bake for approximately 10 more minutes or until crisp and golden brown.

### TO PREPARE THE APPLES:

Peel, core, and cut each apple into 8 sections. Brown the tablespoon of butter in a medium sauté pan over high heat, add the apple wedges, toss to coat with the butter, and sprinkle with the evaporated cane juice. Sauté for about 2 minutes, allowing the evaporated cane juice to caramelize onto the apple wedges. Toss the apple wedges occasionally. Set aside and cool.

### TO PREPARE THE SAUCE:

Place the evaporated cane juice in a small sauce pan and place over high heat. Cook, shaking the pan often, until the cane juice melts and caramelizes to a golden brown. Watch carefully, as the diffcrence between golden brown and burned is only a matter of seconds. Add the heavy cream and boil about 1 minute until the caramel melts and the sauce thickens enough to coat a spoon.

### TO COMPLETE THE NAPOLEON:

Cover one sheet of puff pastry with the apple wedges. Top with a second layer of dough and cover with apples. Cover with the last layer of dough. Warm for 2-3 minutes in a 250 degree oven.

### TO SERVE:

Pour the caramel sauce around the Napoleons and add a scoop of cinnamon ice cream or cinnamon flavored crème fraiche.

# Tête-à-tête

The dictionary defines tête-à-tête as "in intimate privacy" or "together without the intrusion of a third person."

Give the gift of time alone—just the two of you—with the promise of a romantic meal. Imagine the luxurious isolation. I should warn you, passion might literally erupt following such a meal.

Whether an intimate lunch or a pre-theater repast, the selections in this chapter are either prepare-ahead items such as the Coq Au Vin or dishes that require only a short time to finish and present. Why not prepare these dishes together for the ultimate tête-à-tête? Remember, love begins in the kitchen.

# Suggested Menus

◆◆◆

Onion Tart
Chicken in Champagne Sauce
Meringue Glacé


Mille-Feuille of Potato and Smoked Fish
Ragout of Baby Vegetables
Cinnamon Mousse


Claw Meat Crab Cakes
Steak Café de Paris
Rhubarb Crème Brûlée


Seafood Sauerkraut
Monkfish with Radishes
Winter Citrus Salad


Shrimp with Garlic and Herb Butter
Poached Halibut with Sea Vegetables
Frozen Kirsch Soufflés

# Onion Tart

*Both ancient Greeks and Romans believed onions improved sexual performance. The Roman poet Marcus Valerius Martialis, known as Martial wrote in the first century A.D.: "If your wife is old and your member is exhausted, eat onions in plenty."*

THE FILLING:

>   2 tablespoons butter
>   2 cups thinly sliced onions (approximately 2 medium onions)
>   Sea salt
>   Freshly ground pepper

THE TART:

>   1 7-inch Savory Pie Crust (page 248)
>   2 large whole eggs
>   1 egg yolk
>   $1^1/_2$ cups heavy whipping cream
>   1 teaspoon salt
>   $^1/_4$ teaspoon freshly ground pepper
>   $^1/_4$ teaspoon nutmeg
>   Pinch of Cayenne pepper

## TO PREPARE THE ONIONS:

Melt the butter in a small heavy saucepan over low heat. Add the onions and cook slowly until golden brown, 30-40 minutes, stirring often (scraping the bottom of the pan to prevent scorching).

Set aside to cool. Approximately $^1/_2$ cup of cooked onions should remain.

Onions may be prepared the day before and held covered in refrigerator.

## TO PREPARE THE TART:

*Preheat oven to 350 degrees.*

Prebake the pie crust.

Beat the eggs and egg yolk in a glass or stainless steel bowl. Whisk in the heavy cream. Stir in the cooled onions. Add the seasonings and adjust to taste. Fill the pie shell with the mixture and bake in preheated oven until the custard is set and nicely browned, approximately 25 minutes. Test for doneness by inserting a toothpick into the custard. The custard is set if the toothpick comes out clean. Serve warm.

# Mille-Feuille of Potato and Smoked Fish

Mille-Feuille, *French for "a thousand leaves" is a dessert made by sandwiching thin sheets of puff pastry with layers of jam or pastry cream. This savory version uses thin slices of roasted potato instead of the traditional puff pastry.*

    2 large Russet potatoes
    2 tablespoons olive oil
    4 ounces assorted smoked fish: salmon, tuna, trout, etc.
    1 large egg
    2 teaspoons finely chopped herbs: parsley, chives, or tarragon
    1 tablespoon bread crumbs
    1 tablespoon grated Parmesan cheese
    1 tablespoon butter
    Sea salt
    Freshly ground pepper

Peel the potatoes. Cut lengthwise to obtain 8 $1/8$-inch slices of approximately the same size with a mandoline or sharp knife. Immediately cook the potato slices to prevent darkening as follows:

Bring a wide saucepan of salted water to a boil, add the olive oil, and cook the potato slices for about 5 minutes or until just cooked through. Transfer onto a towel to drain completely.

May be prepared several hours ahead to this point.

*Preheat the oven to 425 degrees.*

Beat the egg in a small bowl and whisk in the chopped herbs. Season with freshly ground pepper. As the smoked fish is salted, no extra salt should be required.

Mix the bread crumbs and grated cheese in a small bowl.

If the smoked fish is not pre-sliced, chill in the freezer for about 15 minutes and thinly slice $1/16$-$1/8$-inch thick.

## TO ASSEMBLE THE MILLE-FEUILLES:

Butter a small baking pan or shallow oven proof dish.

Place 2 slices of potato on the baking pan. Brush the potato slices with the egg and herb mixture and cover with a slice of smoked fish. Brush the fish with the egg mixture and cover with a slice of potato. Repeat to obtain 3 layers.

Brush the top slice of potato with the egg mixture and cover with the bread crumb and grated cheese mixture.

Bake the 2 Mille-Feuilles for approximately 5 minutes to warm through and brown the grated cheese.

## TO SERVE:

Place the Mille-Feuilles on warm serving plates.

*Hint:* No sauce is necessary, however, several small dollops of herbed (parsley, chives, tarragon, dill) crème fraîche or sour cream around the plate make a nice garnish. Smoked mussels, scallops, or shrimp also make interesting garnishes.

# Claw Meat Crab Cakes with Celery Root Salad

*This recipe is courtesy of my longtime friend and fishing partner Lance Gilbert who was raised on Maryland's Eastern Shore.*

THE CELERY ROOT SALAD:

> 1 medium celery root
> $1/2$ cup Mayonnaise (page 245)
> $1/2$ teaspoon dry mustard
> Pinch of evaporated cane juice or sugar
> $1/2$ teaspoon lemon juice
> Sea salt
> Freshly ground pepper

THE CRAB CAKES:

> 8 ounces claw crab meat
> 1 small egg
> 1 tablespoon minced shallots
> $1/2$ teaspoon Old Bay seasoning
> 4 tablespoons mayonnaise
> 1 teaspoon freshly grated lemon zest
> 1 teaspoon lemon juice
> Pinch of saffron

## TO PREPARE THE CELERY ROOT SALAD:

Peel celery root and cut into a julienne, the size of match sticks. In a bowl, mix mayonnaise with dry mustard, lemon juice, salt, and pepper. Gently toss the julienned celery root with the other ingredients until well coated. Taste and adjust seasonings.

## TO PREPARE THE CRAB CAKES:

*Preheat the oven to 400 degrees.*

Remove any pieces of shell that remain in the crab meat.

Place the picked crab meat in a bowl. Beat the egg to a light foam in a mixing bowl and add the other ingredients, mixing thoroughly. Add the crab last, tossing gently to retain large lumps of meat.

Form 2 crab cakes with the prepared meat.

Lightly oil a small baking sheet and arrange the crab cakes on it. Bake for about 12 minutes in the preheated oven until the crab cakes are hot throughout.

Or melt 1 tablespoon of butter in a medium sauté pan on medium heat. Add the crab cakes as the butter just begins to brown. Brown nicely on both sides.

## TO SERVE:

Place 2 tablespoons of celery-root remoulade on each serving plate. Place the crab cakes over the celery root and serve immediately.

*Variation:* Make small bite-sized crab cakes. Place on rice crackers to serve as appetizers .

*Hint:* Celery root or celeriac is found only during the fall and winter months.

# Seafood Sauerkraut

*Dr. Weston Price, author of* Nutrition and Physical Degeneration, *traveled the world, studying so-called primitive people and their native diets. In his book, he states that those who had access to seafood had the best health.*

> 2 slices smoked salmon and/or sturgeon
> 2-3 ounces smoked trout
> 4 medium smoked shrimp and/or scallops
> 2-3 ounces firm white fish: monkfish, rockfish, etc.
> 2-4 small red bliss potatoes
> $\frac{1}{2}$ cup cooked sauerkraut
> 3-4 tablespoons dry white wine
> $\frac{1}{3}$ cup White Butter Sauce (page 233)

Prepare the fish by skinning and removing any small bones from the smoked fish. Cut the fillets into 2 portions; sections should be approximately $\frac{1}{2}$-inch thick.

Boil the potatoes in a pot of salted water until tender, about 15 minutes.

## TO PREPARE THE DISH:

Spread the cooked and seasoned sauerkraut in a small 6-8 inch saucepan. Pour in the 3-4 tablespoons of dry Alsatian wine. If the sauerkraut is rather moist, 3 tablespoons should be enough. Place the fresh and smoked fish on top of the sauerkraut and bring to a boil over high heat. Cover and reduce to low flame to cook fresh fish and heat the smoked fish. Turn the fish after 2 minutes and cook about another 2-3 minutes.

Once the fish is just cooked through, mound the sauerkraut in the center of two serving plates. Arrange fish on and around the sauerkraut with the boiled potatoes.

Serve immediately with the white butter sauce poured around the fish.

*Hint:* Just about any combination of fresh and smoked seafood will do. Go for whatever is in season. Double the above recipe for two main courses.

If you find uncooked sauerkraut at a farmer's market, you need to cook it using the recipe below:

> 1 pound sauerkraut
> 2 tablespoons oil
> ½ cup finely slivered onions
> 1 cup dry white wine
> 1 *bouquet garni* consisting of 1 small bay leaf, 1 clove, 1 clove
>     of garlic crushed, pinch of thyme, 3 crushed juniper berries,
>     and 3-4 cracked black peppercorns, wrapped in cheesecloth.

## TO PREPARE THE SAUERKRAUT:

*Preheat the oven to 350 degrees.*

Place the sauerkraut in a strainer and rinse with cold water.

Press the sauerkraut to remove as much moisture as possible.

Heat the oil in a heavy saucepan, add the onions and simmer until limp, but do not brown. Add the sauerkraut, pinch of salt, wine, and *bouquet garni* and bring to a boil.

Cover, transfer to the oven and cook for about 1 hour. The sauerkraut should remain somewhat crisp. Remove from oven; taste and adjust seasonings.

# Shrimp with Garlic and Herb Butter

*The herb butter may be prepared ahead and even frozen until ready to use.*

THE HERB BUTTER:

> $1/2$ pound lightly salted butter
> 1 tablespoon finely chopped parsley
> 1 teaspoon lemon juice
> 1 drop of Tabasco sauce
> $1/2$ teaspoon Worcestershire sauce
> $1/2$ teaspoon freshly ground pepper
> $1/2$ teaspoon sea salt
> $1/2$ teaspoon finely chopped shallots
> $1/2$ teaspoon finely chopped garlic

THE SHRIMP:

> $1/2$ pound raw shrimp (8-10 pieces)
> 1 tablespoon butter
> 2 tablespoons dry white wine

## BEGIN BY PREPARING THE HERB BUTTER:

Soften the butter at room temperature for 1 hour. Whip the butter and all the other ingredients together with an electric mixer, food processor, or with a wire whisk. Cover and refrigerate until time to use.

## TO PREPARE THE SHRIMP:

*Preheat the oven to broil.*

Peel and devein the shrimp.

Butter a flameproof baking dish, just large enough to accommodate the shrimp in a single layer, with the 1 tablespoon of butter. Arrange the shrimp; lightly salt and pepper. Add the white wine, place over direct heat and bring to a boil. After the wine boils, turn the shrimp over, allow to cook for less than 1 minute, and remove from heat. Be careful not to overcook.

Dot the shrimp with 2 tablespoons of the garlic and herb butter and place under the broiler until the butter melts. Serve at once.

*Variation:* Substitute lobster tails or prawns.

# Ragout of Baby Vegetables

*The thought of a hearty ragout stimulates my appetite. Ragout is a lustly-seasoned stew made from meat, poultry or game with vegetables, cooked in a thickened liquid. This is my vegetarian version.*

THE SAUCE:

> $^1/_2$ cup packed morel or shiitake mushrooms (2 ounces)
> 1 teaspoon olive oil or butter
> $^1/_2$ teaspoon finely chopped shallots
> 1 cup Chicken Stock (page 239) or Aromatic Broth (page 237)
> Sea salt
> Freshly ground pepper

THE RAGOUT:

> 2 tablespoons olive oil or butter
> 8 morel or shiitake mushrooms (2 ounces)
> 1 teaspoon finely minced shallots
> 6 miniature baby zucchini, stemmed (4 ounces)
> 6 baby carrots, tops trimmed, peeled (4 ounces)
> 14 haricots verts, trimmed
> 10 sugar snap peas
> 10 small asparagus
> 6 baby turnips (4 ounces)
> 6 baby onions

## TO PREPARE THE SAUCE:

Trim the stems and split the morel mushrooms in half. Soak in a bowl of cold water for a few minutes. Pull the mushrooms out of the water, leaving the grit behind. Repeat cleaning procedure. Drain well.

Place the butter in a saucepan over high heat. Just as the butter begins to brown, add the drained mushrooms and shallots. Sauté for about 1 minute tossing once or twice. Season with sea salt and freshly ground pepper.

Add the chicken stock or aromatic broth and bring to a boil over high heat. Reduce the liquid by a third (about 3 minutes).

Pour contents in a small food processor and puree. Transfer to a cup or small bowl. Adjust seasonings and set aside.

## TO PREPARE THE RAGOUT:

Heat the oil in a medium saucepan over moderate heat.

Add the mushrooms and shallots. Toss once or twice and add the remaining vegetables, except the snow or sugar snap peas.

Sauté the vegetables for 2 minutes, tossing several times.

Add the sauce and toss to evenly coat the vegetables. Reduce heat, cover and simmer for 10-12 minutes, until the vegetables are the desired doneness, stirring frequently. I prefer them with a bit of crunch. Add the peas 1 minute before the other vegetables are ready. Taste and adjust seasonings.

Serve with a grain such as couscous or brown rice, if desired.

*Hint:* Try other seasonal vegetables, such as Japanese eggplant, fiddlehead ferns, young greens, kohlrabi, etc.

# Sea Bass with Clam Vinaigrette

*An enticingly easy dish to prepare. Fresh herbs make all the difference. Practitioners of folk medicine recommend crushing parsley stems and rubbing the juice onto insect stings for quick relief.*

8-12 ounces of skinless sea bass fillet
12 little neck clams
$1/2$ cup minced red bell pepper
$1/4$ cup diced tomato
1 teaspoon finely chopped fresh herbs (parsley, cilantro
   or chives)
1 teaspoons finely diced Klamata olives
1 teaspoon minced shallots
1 tablespoon extra virgin olive oil
2 teaspoons fresh lemon juice
1 tablespoon dry vermouth
Sea salt
Freshly ground pepper
Pinch of cayenne

Cut the sea bass into very thin diagonal slices and arrange in a flower-like design (concentric circles) on two oven proof plates. Cover the plates with plastic wrap and refrigerate.

Steam open the clams (overcooking will toughen them), and remove from shells. Reserve clams in their cooking juices and refrigerate.

## PREPARE THE VINAIGRETTE:

Place the shallots, chopped herbs, diced olives, diced tomato and pepper in a small bowl. Add the olive oil, lemon juice, vermouth, salt, pepper, and cayenne, mixing carefully. Taste and adjust the seasonings.

## TO SERVE:

Warm the vinaigrette in a double boiler and add the drained clams. Place the plates of fish under a preheated broiler for approximately 30 seconds, until the fish is warmed through. Spoon the vinaigrette over the sea bass and serve.

Garnish with fresh cilantro or tarragon and sprinkle lightly with more sea salt.

# Poached Halibut
# with Sea Vegetables

*Brillat-Savarin, French culinary philosopher, states that seafood "acts strongly on the genetic sense, and awakes in both sexes the instincts of reproduction." Sea vegetables, unjustly called "weeds," contain the vital trace minerals so important to optimum health.*

> 1 recipe Aromatic Broth (without salt) (page 237)
> 1-2 ounces assorted sea vegetables: kelp, nori, wakame, dulse
> 10-12 ounces halibut fillet

Prepare the aromatic broth without salt.

Cut the sea vegetables that require cooking into bite-sized pieces with the aid of heavy kitchen scissors.

Heat the strained aromatic broth, add the prepared sea vegetables, and poach until tender. Cook each type of sea vegetable separately as each requires different cooking time.

Remove the cooked sea vegetables from the broth and set aside.

Cut the halibut fillet into 2 pieces. Bring the aromatic broth to a boil over high heat and poach the fish for approximately 3-4 minutes or until just cooked through. Remove the fish from the broth with the aid of a slotted spatula and place in 2 large shallow serving bowls. Taste and adjust seasonings of the court bouillon. Pour approximately 2 ounces of the broth over the fish and add the sea vegetables to each of the bowls. Serve immediately.

# Rockfish with a Wild Mushroom Crust

*The mushroom crust begins with Duxelles, a basic preparation of chopped mushrooms and shallots sautéed in butter. Seasoned bread crumbs are used to bind the prepared mushrooms, forming the crust.*

THE MUSHROOM CRUST:

> 1 tablespoon butter
> 1 packed cup, 6 ounces wild mushrooms (single or assorted)
> 1 tablespoon finely minced shallots
> ½ teaspoon lemon juice
> Sea salt
> Freshly ground pepper
> Pinch of *Herbs de Provence* or chopped fresh thyme
> 2 tablespoons bread crumbs

THE FISH:

> 2 4-6 ounce rockfish fillets
> 2 tablespoons butter
> 2 teaspoons of finely minced shallots
> ⅔ cup dry white wine or Aromatic Broth (page 237)
> Sea salt
> Freshly ground pepper
> 2 tablespoons Chive Oil (page 244)

## TO PREPARE THE MUSHROOM CRUST:

Thoroughly wash, drain and finely chop the wild mushrooms.

In a large saucepan, melt the butter, add shallots, chopped mushrooms and lemon juice, and reduce over medium heat until the mushroom juices evaporate. The chopped mushrooms should be only slightly moist. Remove from heat and stir in the bread crumbs and herbs. Season with salt and pepper. Reserve. May be prepared 1 day ahead.

*TO ASSEMBLE:*

*Preheat the oven to 425 degrees.*

Butter a baking pan large enough to hold the fillets and sprinkle with the shallots. Place the rockfish fillets on the shallots and lightly season with salt and pepper. Coat the fillets with the wild mushroom crust. Pour the white wine around the fish, approximately $1/4$ inch deep. Place the pan on the stove over high heat and bring to a boil. Transfer to the oven and bake for 8-10 minutes until the fish is just cooked through.

Place the fillets on a warm serving platter or individual plates. Pour about 1 tablespoon of the Chive Oil around the fish and serve immediately.

Garnish with whole sautéed wild mushrooms, if desired.

# Grouper Braised in Beer with Chanterelles

*Chanterelles are mushrooms found in forests of the Pacific Northwest. More durable than other mushroom varieties, golden Chanterelles, known as "queens of the forest," are ideal for sautéing.*

> 1½ tablespoons butter
> 1 teaspoon finely chopped shallots
> 3-4 ounces Chanterelles mushrooms
> ½ cup lager beer
> 8-10 ounces grouper fillet, ½-inch thick
> ½ teaspoon Dijon-style mustard
> ½ cup heavy whipping cream
> Sea salt
> Freshly ground pepper

Cut the grouper fillet into two portions.

Wash and trim the Chanterelles mushrooms, cutting any large ones in half. Drain completely.

Place the butter in a medium shallow saucepan and place over high heat. When the butter begins to foam, add the shallots and spread around the pan with a spoon. Immediately add the mushrooms, season with salt and pepper and sauté for about 1 minute, tossing often.

Add the 2 portions of grouper and pour in the beer. Bring to a boil, reduce heat, cover, and simmer for 3 minutes, until the fish is just cooked through. Transfer the fish to a serving platter with the aid of a slotted spatula, cover. Leave the mushrooms in the pan.

Return the pan to high heat, bring to a boil, and reduce the liquid by a third. Add the mustard and heavy cream and bring to a boil. Remove from heat. Taste and adjust seasonings.

## TO SERVE:

Place the covered serving platter of grouper in a 350 degree oven for about 4 minutes to heat. Remove from oven. Transfer the mushrooms around the fish and spoon the sauce over the grouper. Serve immediately.

*Variation:* Use Morel, Shiitake or other mushrooms in place of the Chanterelles. If using dried mushrooms, soak overnight and change water several times before using. Substitute Red Snapper or Sea Bass.

# Cobia with Ramps

*Early settlers treasured ramps, one of the first vegetables to arrive in the spring. Ramps or wild leeks, as they are called, are wild onions that resemble scallions with broad tulip-like leaves. Ramps have an assertive, garlicky-onion flavor and are eaten raw or cooked. They may replace leeks, scallions, or onions in other dishes.*

10-12 ounces Cobia fillet, about $1/2$-inch thick
Sea salt
Freshly ground pepper
1 tablespoon butter
1 teaspoon olive oil
12-18 small ramps, the size of a pencil

THE SAUCE:

2 tablespoons white wine vinegar or apple cider vinegar
$1/2$ cup white wine
$1/2$ teaspoon finely minced shallots
2 tablespoons butter
Sea salt
Freshly ground pepper

## TO PREPARE THE RAMPS:

Trim the root end just prior to using and strip off any loose filmy outer skin that may be present.

Cut away the leaves about $1/2$-1 inch above where the green stem starts.

Remove any brown edges from the leaves.

## TO PREPARE THE FISH AND SAUCE:

Lightly salt and pepper the fish. Place a medium sauté pan over high heat and add the butter and oil. When the butter just begins to brown, add the seasoned fish, serving side down.

Reduce heat to medium and brown the fillet, about 2 minutes.

Flip the 2 fillets over and add the prepared ramps, placing them to the sides of the fish. Cover the pan and cook for about 2 more minutes until the fish is just cooked through. Shake the pan 2-3 times to coat the ramps with the butter while the fish is cooking.

Remove fish and ramps to a serving platter, placing the fish over the ramps. Cover and keep warm.

Pour the butter/oil out of the pan. Add the vinegar, white wine, shallots, pinch of salt, and 2-3 turns of the pepper mill. Place the pan over high heat and bring to a boil. Reduce liquid by about two-thirds and remove from heat. Whisk in the 2 tablespoons butter and taste and adjust seasonings. Spoon the sauce over the fish and ramps.

*Variation:* Substitute grouper or snapper. Use spring onions in place of the ramps.

# Monkfish with Radishes

*Indigenous to China, the radish made its way to Asia Minor where the Greeks used it to worship Apollo and the Romans introduced it to the Germans. Curry powder is a blend of ingredients and usually contains cardamom seeds, coriander seeds, cumin, garlic, ginger, mustard seeds, and turmeric. This fragrant mélange is a reputed sexual stimulant.*

> 8-10 ounces monkfish fillet
> $\frac{1}{2}$ teaspoon curry powder
> Sea salt
> Freshly ground pepper

THE RADISH SALAD:

> $\frac{1}{2}$ cup finely diced radishes
> $\frac{1}{2}$ cup finely diced Granny Smith apple ($\frac{1}{2}$ apple)
> 1 teaspoon lemon juice
> 2 teaspoons extra virgin olive oil
> Sea salt
> Freshly ground pepper

THE SAUCE:

> 1 bunch of parsley
> 1 teaspoon olive oil
> Sea salt
> Freshly ground pepper

## TO PREPARE THE MONKFISH:

Remove the dark outer skin and translucent gray inner skin, exposing the white flesh. Slice the fillets into $\frac{1}{2}$-inch thick medallions. Set aside.

## TO PREPARE THE RADISH SALAD:

Wash and stem the radishes. Peel the apple. Finely dice the radishes and then the apple and place in a small mixing bowl. Add the lemon juice, olive oil, salt, and pepper and toss thoroughly. Taste and adjust seasonings.

## TO PREPARE THE SAUCE:

Wash the bunch of parsley and blanch by plunging into a pot of boiling salted water for 30 seconds. Transfer blanched parsley to a bowl of cold water. Drain well and juice to obtain $1/2$ cup of parsley juice. Add the olive oil and season with salt and pepper. Heat slightly without boiling.

## TO COOK THE MONKFISH:

Season the monkfish medallions with salt, pepper, and curry. Sear the monkfish medallions in a small sauté pan in olive oil. Cook for about 2 minutes per side until just cooked through. Remove from pan.

## TO SERVE:

Divide the radish/apple salad between 2 serving plates.

Place the monkfish medallions on top of the salad.

Pour the warm parsley juice around the fish.

Garnish the plate with a sprig of fresh parsley and serve.

*Variation:* If you do not have a vegetable juicer, purée the parsley in a blender and strain to obtain the juice. Substitute tarragon or chives for the parsley.

# Fillet of Trout Poached in Beer with Sauerkraut

*Fermented vegetables, especially sauerkraut, have been produced since ancient times. The fermenting process enhances digestibility and the nutritional value of such foods. The great explorer Captain James Cook carried thousands of pounds of health-giving sauerkraut on his second voyage to the South Pacific to preserve the health of his crew.*

2 5-ounce trout fillets
2 teaspoons butter
1 teaspoon finely minced shallots
$1/2$ cup mild beer
2 tablespoons crème fraîche
Sea salt
Freshly ground pepper
1 cup cooked sauerkraut
1 tablespoon chopped chives

Remove any bones or skin from the trout fillets and season with salt and pepper.

Melt but do not brown the butter in a medium sauce pan. Add the minced shallots and the prepared trout fillets.

Immediately pour the beer over the trout fillets and bring to a boil over high heat. Cover and cook for approximately 1 minute until the trout fillets are cooked. Remove the trout from the saucepan with a slotted spatula to a platter. Cover and keep warm.

Heat the sauerkraut in a small pan over low heat and keep warm.

Place the sauce pan over high heat and reduce the liquid by half.

Remove from heat and whisk in the crème fraîche. Taste and adjust seasonings.

## TO SERVE:

Divide the warm sauerkraut between two warm plates and place a trout fillet on top of the sauerkraut.

Pour the sauce around the trout and sprinkle the chopped chives over the trout fillets. Serve with boiled potatoes.

# Chicken in Champagne Sauce with Herb Spätzle

*Spätzle, literally "little sparrow" in German, is a dish of small dumplings. The spätzle can be firm enough to be rolled out and cut into slivers, or soft enough to be forced through a sieve or colander. There are several spellings depending on which side of the Rhine River they originate. Free range chickens are the elite of the poultry world. Instead of mass-produced birds allotted 1 square foot of space, each range chicken has double that area indoors plus the occasional freedom to roam outdoors. They are fed a special diet free of antibiotics, animal byproducts, or growth hormones.*

1 2½-3 pound free range chicken

THE MARINADE:

1½ cups champagne

½ cup finely sliced onions

½ cup finely sliced carrots

½ teaspoon cracked peppercorns

1 clove of garlic peeled and crushed

1 bay leaf

2 cloves

Pinch of thyme

THE CHICKEN SAUCE:

Reserved chicken carcass, plus wing parts, necks, and giblets

2 tablespoons olive oil

½ cup diced onion

½ cup diced carrot

1 rounded tablespoon flour

2 cups cold water

1 bay leaf

1 clove

Pinch of thyme

½ teaspoon sea salt

½ teaspoon freshly ground pepper

THE CHICKEN:

> Sea salt
> Freshly ground pepper
> Flour
> 1 tablespoon butter
> 1 tablespoon olive oil
> 2 tablespoons finely chopped onion
> Marinade, about 1 cup will remain
> $\frac{1}{3}$ cup champagne
> $\frac{1}{2}$ cup chicken stock
> $\frac{1}{3}$ pound fresh white or Shiitake mushrooms

THE HERB SPÄTZLE:

> 1$\frac{1}{2}$ cups sifted fine whole wheat flour
> $\frac{1}{2}$ teaspoon sea salt
> Pinch of freshly ground pepper
> Pinch of freshly grated nutmeg
> 2 tablespoons chopped fresh parsley or tarragon
> 2 whole eggs
> $\frac{1}{8}$ cup water (approximately)
> 2 tablespoons butter

## TO MARINATE THE CHICKEN:

Cut the chicken into quarters, removing the wings at the second joint. Reserve the neck, giblet, carcass, and wing tips.

Combine the marinade ingredients in a bowl. Add the chicken quarters, add more champagne if the chicken is not completely covered. Cover and refrigerate overnight.

## TO PREPARE THE CHICKEN STOCK:

Cut the chicken carcass into 3-4 pieces with a cleaver. In a heavy saucepan or Dutch oven, heat the oil over medium flame. Add all the reserved parts and sauté for about 10 minutes until bones are lightly browned, stirring occasionally. Add the diced vegetables and cook an additional 4-5 minutes.

Dust the bones with the flour and stir thoroughly, scraping the bottom of the pan, and cook for 1 minute. Cover the bones with the water and bring to a boil over high heat. Skim the fat and add the remaining ingredients. Lower the heat and simmer uncovered for approximately 30 minutes to reduce and concentrate the stock. Strain and skim. Approximately $1/2$ cup should remain. If, after straining, more than $1/2$ cup remains, place in a small pot and boil until reduced sufficiently.

## TO PREPARE THE CHICKEN:

Lift the chicken quarters out of the marinade; allow to drain thoroughly in a colander. Strain the marinade reserving only the liquid.

Season the chicken quarters with salt and pepper and dust with flour, shaking off the excess.

Heat the butter and oil in a saucepan or Dutch oven just large enough to hold the chicken quarters on one level. When the butter begins to brown, sauté the chicken quarters for 2-3 minutes per side over high heat to brown lightly.

Remove browned chicken to a platter and pour out the grease.

Add the chopped onion and the mushrooms, cleaned and quartered. Sauté over medium heat for 2 minutes to cook the onion and mushrooms, stirring often. Return the chicken to the pan. Add the red wine and bring to a boil over high heat.

Combine the reserved marinade and chicken stock in a small pan, place on medium heat and bring to a boil, whisking often. Skim well and add to the pot of chicken.

Bring to a boil, reduce heat, cover and simmer for about 15 minutes, occasionally shaking the pot. Test for doneness. Meat should be fork tender. Taste for seasonings.

## TO PREPARE THE SPÄTZLE:

Place the flour in a large mixing bowl with the salt, nutmeg, pepper, and chopped herb. Break the eggs into a bowl and whisk thoroughly. Gradually pour the eggs into the flour, mixing completely by hand with a flexible rubber spatula. Add the water a little at a time and mix until the dough no longer adheres to the sides of the bowl.

The dough should remain rather firm.

Bring 2 quarts of water with 2 tablespoons of salt to a rapid boil. Place the *spätzle* maker or a colander with large holes over the pot of water. Force the dough through the holes with a rubber spatula. Use $\frac{1}{2}$ of the dough at a time. Allow the *spätzle* to cook until they rise to the surface, about 3-4 minutes. Transfer the cooked *spätzle* into a large bowl of cold lightly salted water. Repeat until all the dough is used.

## TO SERVE:

Thoroughly drain the *spätzle* in a colander. Melt the butter in a sauté pan large enough to hold the *spätzle*. When the butter begins to brown, add the *spätzle* and sauté for 1-2 minutes, tossing often, until hot. Taste and adjust seasonings.

Heat the chicken and serve with *spätzle*. Traditionally one tops the *Coq au Vin* with sautéed julienned bacon, pearl onions, and a large heart-shaped crouton.

*Hint:* This type of dish is often better prepared ahead and reheated but be careful not to overcook the chicken. White or red wine may be used in place of the champagne to produce a traditional *Coq au Vin*. Noodles are a fine substitute for the *spätzle*.

# Steak Café de Paris
# with Potatoes Boulangère

*The term "Boulangère" harkens back to a time when the baker might have the only suitable oven in the entire village. Dishes were dropped off by the villagers to be baked along with the bread.*

### THE POTATOES BOULANGÈRE:

> 1 large Russet potato, 8-10 ounces
> 1 medium onion, 1 1/2 cups sliced
> 2 tablespoons butter
> 1 tablespoon olive oil
> 1/2 teaspoon chopped fresh thyme
> Sea salt
> Freshly ground pepper
> 1 1/2 cups White Stock (page 228) or Aromatic Broth (page 237)

### THE STEAKS:

> 2 8-10 ounce strip steaks
> 1 tablespoon butter
> 1 tablespoon extra virgin olive oil
> Sea salt
> Freshly ground pepper
> 1 tablespoon butter

### THE SAUCE:

> 2 teaspoons finely minced shallots
> 1 teaspoon finely chopped parsley
> 1/2 teaspoon finely chopped tarragon
> 1/4 teaspoon finely chopped garlic
> 4 tablespoons crème fraîche
> Sea salt
> Freshly ground pepper

### *TO PREPARE THE POTATOES:*

Peel and thinly slice the onion. Heat the butter and oil in a heavy saucepan. When the butter begins to brown, add the sliced onions. Cook over medium heat until golden brown, stirring often, about 20 minutes. Remove from heat and pour out excess fat. Season lightly with salt and pepper. Allow to cool.

49

Peel the potato, cut in half lengthwise, and thinly slice (⅛-inch). Combine the sliced potato and browned onions in a bowl. Season with salt, pepper, and thyme and toss to thoroughly mix.

Transfer the mixture to a small baking dish, approximately 6-inch x 6-inch x 2½-inches. Barely cover the mixture with your choice of seasoned broth. The potatoes will give off water so just add broth to the level of the mixture.

Bake in a 425 degree preheated oven for about 35 minutes until the potatoes are tender and turning brown on top.

Test for doneness by piercing a potato slice with a fork.

Serve hot.

*Hint:* Substitute vegetable broth for the beef broth for a vegetarian version. May even be prepared with water. The potatoes may be prepared ahead and reheated.

## TO PREPARE THE STEAKS:

Place the butter and oil in a heavy cast iron skillet over high heat.

Salt and pepper the steaks.

When the butter begins to brown, add the steaks and sauté until browned on both sides, approximately 2-3 minutes per side for medium rare.

Remove steaks and place on a serving platter, keeping them warm while preparing the sauce.

Pour the butter and oil out of the pan in which the steaks were cooked.

Place the pan over medium heat and add the tablespoon of butter.

When the butter has just melted, add the minced shallots and allow to cook for 10 seconds without browning. Add the chopped herbs and garlic and cook for another 10 seconds, stirring once or twice.

Add the crème fraîche and heat, stirring once or twice without boiling.

Taste and adjust seasonings and pour over the cooked steaks.

Serve with Potatoes Boulangère.

# Osso Bucco Braised in Beer with Brown Rice Pilaf

*I prefer these Alsatian-style braised veal shanks simmered in a dark or stout beer for the rich malty taste. Prepare the shanks up to two days ahead and reheat just before serving. The brown rice is tastier and nutritionally superior to the refined product.*

THE VEAL:

>2 pieces of veal shank, each approximately $1\frac{1}{2}$ inches thick
>Sea salt
>Freshly ground pepper
>1 tablespoon flour
>2 tablespoons olive oil
>1 rounded tablespoon chopped onion
>1 rounded tablespoon chopped carrot
>1 level tablespoon chopped celery
>1 cup of dark beer
>1 bay leaf
>1 clove
>Pinch of coarsely ground pepper
>1 crushed clove of garlic
>$\frac{1}{2}$ teaspoon Pâté Spices (page 228)
>$\frac{1}{2}$ cup Veal or Beef Sauce (page 232)

THE RICE PILAF:

>2 tablespoons butter
>3 tablespoons onion, finely chopped
>$\frac{1}{2}$ cup brown rice
>1 clove
>1 very small bay leaf
>$\frac{1}{2}$ teaspoon salt
>Dash freshly ground pepper
>1 cup Chicken Stock (page 239)

## TO PREPARE THE SHANKS:

*Preheat oven to 425 degrees.*

Season the veal shanks with salt and pepper and dust lightly with flour.

Heat the oil in an ovenproof casserole just large enough to hold the veal shanks in one layer. Brown the shanks well on both sides over high heat. Add the chopped onion, carrot, and celery; cover and cook for 2-3 minutes, shaking the casserole once or twice.

Remove casserole from the heat and carefully pour off any excess fat.

Pour the beer into the casserole and return to high heat. Bring beer to a boil; add garlic, spices, and veal stock. Bring liquid to a boil, cover the casserole, and place in a preheated 425 degree oven. Braise for approximately 1 hour and 15 minutes or until the shanks are very tender. Strain the sauce, adjust seasonings, and pour over the shanks. While the shanks are braising, prepare the rice.

## TO PREPARE THE RICE:

*Preheat oven to 375 degrees.*

In a small ovenproof saucepan, melt but do not brown 1 tablespoon of the butter. Add the onions and cook over low heat about 4 minutes, stirring occasionally.

Pour in the rice and mix well. Add the clove, bay leaf, salt and pepper. Cover rice with the broth to a level of $1/3$ inch above the rice. Bring to a boil, cover and put in the oven for about 35 minutes or until tender and liquid has been absorbed. Fold in remaining butter with a fork. Adjust seasonings and serve.

To serve: Place a portion of brown rice in the center of 2 warm plates and place the shanks and sauce over the rice.

# Winter Citrus Salad
# with Chocolate Ice Cream
# and Honey Sauce

*The story goes that when Cesar Ritz wanted to purchase the Parisian palace that became the Ritz, he obtained the funds from the Marnier family. Marnier later acquired the rights to an orange liqueur and asked Ritz what to name the liqueur. Ritz replied "call it Grand Marnier." My Great Uncle Jacques worked for M. Ritz and the famous chef August Escouffier at the London Ritz Hotel.*

## THE SAUCE:

> 1 large orange
> 2 tablespoons honey
> 2 teaspoons Grand Marnier or orange liqueur

## THE SALAD:

> 2 large oranges
> 1 large grapefruit
> 2 scoops chocolate ice cream
> 1 tablespoon orange or grapefruit rinds

## TO PREPARE THE HONEY SAUCE:

> Press the orange to obtain $1/2$ cup of juice.
> Place the orange juice and honey in a blender and process for a few seconds. Add the Grand Marnier.

## TO PREPARE THE CITRUS:

> Using a sharp knife, cut away the outer rind and white membrane of both the oranges and grapefruit. Section the citrus by cutting along the longitudinal membranes with a sharp knife.

Alternate orange and grapefruit sections around the inside of two serving bowls. Pour the sauce over the fruit.

Place a scoop of chocolate ice cream into the center of each plate and sprinkle the slivered candied orange or grapefruit rinds over the ice cream and fruit. Serve at once.

# Fall Fruit in Spiced Red Wine

*Though once associated with Venus, the goddess of love, and prized as a token of affection, the quince is now typically used for preserves and jelly. Quince, one of my favorite fruits, are available only in the fall.*

THE SPICED WINE:

> 1 orange
> 2 cups red wine
> $\frac{1}{2}$ cup evaporated cane juice or honey
> 1 clove
> $\frac{1}{2}$ bay leaf
> 2 cracked peppercorns
> $\frac{1}{4}$ teaspoon finely chopped ginger or pinch of ginger powder
> $\frac{1}{4}$ teaspoon ground cinnamon
> $\frac{1}{2}$ teaspoon vanilla extract

THE FRUIT:

> 1 apple
> 1 pear
> 1 quince
> 1 tablespoon lemon juice

With the aid of a potato peeler, remove $\frac{1}{2}$ of the skin of the orange. Press the orange to obtain the juice.

In a heavy saucepan, combine the wine and the evaporated cane juice, stirring to dissolve. Add the orange juice, orange zest, clove, bay leaf, pepper, ginger, cinnamon, and vanilla extract.

Bring to a boil, reduce heat, and simmer for about 10 minutes to infuse the spices into the wine. While the wine is simmering prepare the fruit.

Peel and quarter the apple, pear, and quince. Place in a bowl and toss with the lemon juice.

Add the prepared apple, pear and quince to the saucepan containing the wine. Simmer the fruit in the wine for approximately 5 minutes until just cooked through.

Remove the fruit sections from the wine with the aid of a slotted spoon and arrange in a serving bowl.

Reduce the wine by half over high heat and strain the syrup over the fruit. Serve chilled.

# Rhubarb Crème Brûlée

*This is one of my personal favorites. Folk medicine considered rhubarb a spring tonic. It contains phosphorus, potassium, magnesium, iron, and vitamins. The subtle flavor of the rhubarb enhances the creamy custard.*

> 5-6 stalks of rhubarb (6-8 ounces)
> $1/2$ cup evaporated cane juice or sugar

THE CUSTARD:

> 2 large eggs
> $1/2$ cup heavy whipping cream
> $1/2$ vanilla bean or $1/2$ teaspoon vanilla extract
> Pinch of sea salt
> 3-4 tablespoons evaporated cane juice or sugar

THE GARNISH:

> 4 strawberries
> 4 mint leaves

SPECIAL EQUIPMENT:

> 2 1-cup size gratin dishes

## TO PREPARE THE RHUBARB:

Trim the ends and lightly peel the outermost filaments of the stalks. Split the prepared stalks down the center lengthwise and cut into $1/4$-$1/2$-inch dice. Approximately $1 1/3$ cups should remain.

Place the diced rhubarb in a small bowl and mix thoroughly with the sweetener. Cover and refrigerate overnight.

## TO PREPARE THE CUSTARD:

*Preheat oven to 275 degrees.*

The following day, place the prepared rhubarb in a strainer set over a bowl to collect the juice. Use a rubber spatula to scrape all of the juice out of the bowl. Allow the rhubarb to drain for 15 minutes, tossing occasionally.

Transfer the strained juice to a 1-quart size saucepan and place over high heat. Bring the juice to a boil, reduce heat, and continue boiling to reduce by half to a thick syrup, about 4 minutes.

Tilt pan occasionally to avoid scorching. When the syrup is reduced, immediately add the heavy cream and vanilla bean, split, and bring to a low boil. Remove from heat and add the pinch of salt. Allow to steep 2 minutes and remove the vanilla bean.

Beat the eggs in a medium glass or stainless steel bowl.

Slowly pour in the scalded cream, whisking constantly.

If not using vanilla bean, add $1/2$ teaspoon vanilla extract.

Divide the diced rhubarb between the 2 gratin dishes, covering the bottoms. Carefully pour prepared custard over rhubarb.

Set the gratin dishes into a shallow baking dish or pan, at least one inch deep. Fill the gratin dishes with the custard mix. Pour hot tap water into the baking dish to a level halfway up the sides of the gratin dishes.

Place the baking dish in the preheated 275 degree oven and bake until the custard is set, about 35 minutes. Test for doneness by inserting a toothpick into the custard; custard is set if toothpick comes out clean. Allow to cool completely and refrigerate.

## TO FINISH THE CRÈME BRÛLÉE:

Remove from refrigerator about $1/2$ hour before serving, as crème brûlée is best served at room temperature.

*Preheat the broiler.*

Thinly cover each dish with $1 1/2$-2 tablespoons of evaporated cane juice, sugar, or brown sugar. Raise the oven rack as high as possible and place the prepared custards under the broiler. Melt and lightly brown the sweetener, about 1 minute. Pay close attention, as the sweetener burns very quickly. Serve immediately.

Garnish with small whole or large sliced strawberries and mint leaves.

# Cinnamon Mousse

*Cinnamon was among the first commodities traded regularly from the east to the Mediterranean. During Roman times, cinnamon was worth more than its weight in gold. Used in Oriental folk medicine to disinfect minor cuts and relieve pain, cinnamon is the dried inner bark of an Asian evergreen tree of the laurel family. It is peeled from the tree's shoots during the rainy season when the sap is rising. On drying, the bark rolls up into sticks. It is best to grind the cinnamon sticks yourself to get the most flavor.*

> 1 tablespoon honey
> $1/2$ teaspoon gelatin
> 1 tablespoon water
> $1/2$ teaspoon freshly ground cinnamon
> Pinch of sea salt
> 1 teaspoon vanilla extract
> $1 1/2$ teaspoons rum
> 1 cup of heavy whipping cream

Place the honey, gelatin, and water in a small mixing bowl, allowing gelatin to soften for 5 minutes and set over a pot of boiling water. Heat for 1-2 minutes until the gelatin melts. Whisk thoroughly. Remove from heat and add the cinnamon and pinch of salt and mix completely. Pour in the vanilla extract and the rum, blending well.

Whip the heavy cream in a chilled medium mixing bowl and then refrigerate.

Fold the cinnamon mixture into the heavy whipping cream with the aid of a rubber spatula.

Pipe or spoon the mousse into $1/2$-cup size or larger stemware or dishes. Top the mousse with a pinch of cinnamon or a cinnamon stick, if desired.

*Variation:* Substitute freshly ground nutmeg, especially around the holidays.

# Frozen Kirsch Soufflés

*Kirsch is a fruit brandy distilled from cherries.* Eau de vie, *literally "water of life," is a group of fruit brandies. Alsatian* eau de vies *are regarded as some of the finest in the world.*

> 2 tablespoons evaporated cane juice or sugar
> 1 whole egg
> 1½ cups heavy whipping cream
> 2½ tablespoons *Kirsch* (cherry brandy)
> 2 6-ounce (⅔ cup) soufflé ramekins
> 2 12 x 3 inch strips of parchment paper
> Butter

## TO MAKE THE SOUFFLÉS:

Place the egg in a glass or stainless steel bowl or double boiler.

Whisk in the evaporated cane juice.

Place over a pan of hot, simmering water or double boiler. Beat continuously, using the whisk to scrape the egg from the sides and bottom of the bowl. Cook for approximately 1 minute until the egg thickens slightly. Set aside.

Whip the heavy whipping cream. Combine *Kirsch* with the egg mixture and gently fold into the heavy cream.

Taste and add more *Kirsch,* if desired. Chill.

## TO ASSEMBLE THE SOUFFLÉ:

Butter the strip of parchment paper. Form a collar around each mold, buttered side in, with the strip of parchment and secure with tape.

Fill the mold to the top of the collar with the mixture and freeze for at least 6 hours or overnight.

## TO SERVE:

Remove the parchment collar and allow to stand at room temperature for about 15 minutes before serving.

Garnish with fresh or brandied cherries.

# Crêpes with Apples Cooked in Beer

*In regions that did not cultivate grapes, beer became the staple beverage. Cooking demonstrations based on beer recipes are some of my most popular.*

> 4 crêpes: (page 251)
> 2 tablespoons butter
> ¹/₂ cup dark beer
> ¹/₂ cup raisins
> ¹/₂ cup maple syrup
> Pinch of cinnamon
> 2 Ginger Gold or Golden Delicious apples

## PREPARE THE CRÊPES:

Peel, quarter, and core the apples. Cut each quarter into 4 pieces.

Melt the butter in a medium sauté pan. When the butter begins to brown, add the prepared apples, beer, raisins, maple syrup, and cinnamon. Lower heat and boil for about 4-5 minutes until apples are tender (cooking time will vary depending upon the ripeness of the apples). Taste and adjust seasonings, add more maple syrup, if desired, and keep warm.

Place the open crêpes on a warm platter and divide the prepared apples among the 4 crêpes.

Fold the crêpes over and pour any excess syrup around the crêpes.

Place in a 350 degree preheated oven for 3-4 minutes until warmed through.

Serve immediately.

Garnish with a tablespoon of crème fraîche.

*Hint:* Crêpes and filling may be prepared the day before and combined when ready to serve.

# Meringue Glacé

*"Glacé" generally refers to frozen desserts. In this dish, the meringues are placed on either side of the ice cream. A berry coulis moistens this meringue "sandwich."*

## THE MERINGUES:

>4 egg whites
>Pinch of sea salt
>$1/2$ teaspoon grated lemon zest
>$1/2$ teaspoon vanilla extract
>$1/2$ cup evaporated cane juice or sugar
>$1/2$ cup Raspberry Sauce (page 253)

Place the egg whites and pinch of salt in the bowl of an electric mixer. Whip on high speed until just foamy white. Add the evaporated cane juice, 1 tablespoon at a time, and continue beating until the meringue mixture forms stiff glossy peaks. Add the zest and vanilla extract. Do not overbeat.

Transfer the mixture to a pastry bag fitted with a medium star tube. Pipe the mixture onto a sheet pan covered with parchment paper, forming shells.

Place the pan in a very low preheated oven (150 degrees). Allow the meringue to remain in the oven until dry, at least 3 hours or overnight. Remove the sheet pan from the oven and allow to cool. Store the meringue shells in an airtight container until ready to use.

## TO SERVE:

Place a scoop of ice cream in the center of a serving plate.

Sandwich the ice cream between two shells, flat side in. Pour the raspberry sauce and serve.

*Hint:* It is impractical to prepare a smaller amount of meringue. This recipe will make about 10 meringue shells.

# Love in the Afternoon

Dining outside on a clear warm afternoon or evening is the perfect scene for these romantic meals. Eating alfresco lends a festive air to a delightful afternoon repast. A simple cookout can turn into a passionate fling with these flavorful dishes.

Perhaps the two of you are heading to a romantic destination and you want to make it a memorable event from the outset. Bring a picnic basket right on the plane with you. Order two glasses of wine and share a "mile high picnic" lovingly prepared to celebrate your escapade together.

These portable dishes feature chilled recipes such as lobster salad that will liven up your spirits no matter where you are. Maybe it's a picnic supper at our world-renown Wolftrap Farm Park before a concert, a romantic boat ride, or even an intimate cookout on your own balcony.

Whatever the setting, enjoy it with your special someone, and make love in the afternoon.

# Suggested Menus

♦♦♦

Papaya and Shrimp Soup
Salmon Rillettes
Strawberry and Rhubarb Salad


Goat Cheese Salad with Sesame Vinaigrette
Beef Carpaccio
Blood Orange Salad


Grilled Vegetable Salad with Carrot Sauce
Marinated Rockfish
Citrus Salad with Ginger


Lobster and Asparagus Salad
Marinated Beef Salad
Spiced Strawberries


Marinated Dill Salmon
Lentil Salad
Frozen Raspberry Soufflés

# Papaya and Shrimp Soup

*In the tropics, papayas have been used medically to reduce fevers, cure toothaches and even remove freckles. Most welcomed on a warm day, this combination is sure to please.*

1 1/2 cups Aromatic Broth (page 237)
12 medium shrimp
1 large ripe papaya
1/2 cup Sauternes or other sweet wine
Sea salt
Freshly ground pepper
Mint

Bring the aromatic broth to a boil over high heat and add the shrimp. When the broth boils again, remove the pan from the heat and set aside allowing the shrimp to remain in the broth. Allow the broth to cool. May be prepared several hours ahead.

Peel, split, and remove seeds from the papaya. Cut the papaya sections in half and set aside 1/4 of the papaya to garnish the plate just before serving.

Place the Sauternes in a small pot, bring to boil over high heat, and reduce by half. Allow to cool.

Cut the prepared papaya, 3/4 of the fruit, into large pieces and place in a food processor. Purée the fruit. Add the cooled Sauternes and process for 2-3 seconds to mix thoroughly. Taste and add a pinch of salt and pepper, if necessary.

Divide the puréed papaya between two serving plates.

Peel the cooled shrimp and divide between the two serving plates. Slice the reserved 1/4 papaya into 4-6 thin slices and place among the shrimp.

Garnish the plates with fresh mint leaves or cilantro.

Prepare ahead and serve lightly chilled.

*Variation:* Prepare with ripe cantaloupe and season with uncooked port wine.

# Goat Cheese Salad
# with Sesame Vinaigrette

*Mesclun or "spring mix" is an upscale combination of baby lettuces and greens. The word is a derivative of French slang meaning "mixture." Sesame seeds are one of the richest sources of calcium, especially if served raw.*

## THE VINAIGRETTE:

    2 anchovy fillets
    3 tablespoons extra virgin olive oil
    1 tablespoon sherry wine vinegar
    1 tablespoon raw sesame seeds (substitute pumpkin or sunflower)
    2 teaspoons capers
    Sea salt
    Freshly ground pepper

## THE SALAD:

    4 large peeled garlic cloves
    2 small slices country bread
    2 ounces mesclun salad (2 cups)
    1 medium red bell pepper
    1 medium ripe tomato
    4 anchovy fillets
    3 ounces goat cheese log

## TO PREPARE THE VINAIGRETTE:

Mash the anchovy fillets in a medium mixing bowl. Add the remaining ingredients and whisk thoroughly. Taste and adjust seasonings

## PREPARE THE GARLIC TOAST:

*Preheat the oven to 325 degrees.*

Place the garlic in a small oven proof pan and roast the garlic until soft and lightly browned, about 20 minutes. Allow to cool slightly. Toast the bread and spread the softened garlic on the toasted bread.

## TO PREPARE THE SALAD:

Wash, split, and remove seeds of the red bell pepper. Cut the bell pepper into a large julienne. Wash and quarter the tomato and cut the chèvre into 6 round slices.

## TO ASSEMBLE:

Place the salad greens in a mixing bowl, add $^3/_4$ of the salad dressing and toss.

Divide the salad between two serving plates.

Arrange 3 slices of chèvre, $^1/_2$ of the bell pepper, and anchovy fillets on the salad. Place the tomato quarters and garlic toasts around the plates. Spoon the remaining vinaigrette over the tomato and bell pepper slices and serve.

*Hint:* Marinated uncooked anchovy fillets are preferred. Substitute 2 teaspoons anchovy paste for the fillets. Use red wine vinegar rather than the sherry wine vinegar.

# Grilled Vegetable Salad with Carrot Sauce

*The Ancient Greeks believed carrots to be aphrodisiacs. The word aphrodisiac is derived from Aphrodite, the Greek goddess of love. That's why I drink a glass of carrot juice every-day and recommend you do the same.*

THE VINAIGRETTE:

        1/3 cup extra virgin olive oil
        1 1/2 tablespoons balsamic vinegar
        1/2 teaspoon Dijon-style mustard
        Sea salt
        Freshly ground pepper
        1/2 teaspoon finely minced chives
        1/2 teaspoon finely chopped parsley
        1/2 teaspoon finely chopped tarragon

THE SALAD:

        1 small zucchini
        1 small yellow squash
        1 medium carrot
        1 large new red potato
        1 medium red or yellow bell pepper
        1 medium tomato
        1 medium red onion
        8 jumbo cloves of unpeeled garlic
        4 ounces salad greens (one handful)

THE SAUCE:

        1/2 cup fresh carrot juice
        Sea salt
        Freshly ground pepper

THE GARNISH:

        Parsley sprigs, tarragon leaves, and chive straws

## *TO PREPARE THE VINAIGRETTE:*

Combine all the ingredients to prepare the vinaigrette. Taste and adjust seasonings.

## TO PREPARE THE VEGETABLES:

Peel, trim the ends, and slice the carrots lengthwise, $1/2$-inch thick. Trim the ends and slice the zucchini and yellow squash into $1/2$-inch thick lengthwise strips.

Wash and dry the potato. Trim, if necessary, and cut into $1/2$-inch thick slices.

Peel the red onion and cut into quarters.

Wash the bell pepper, split in half, and remove the seeds and membrane. Split each half in two. Wash tomato, cut away the stem, and cut in half.

Place the prepared vegetables and the garlic cloves in a shallow dish. Season with salt and pepper and coat lightly with olive oil by tossing gently in the dish.

Wash and thoroughly drain the salad.

*Preheat the grill.*

Sear the seasoned vegetables over a hot grill about 8 minutes.

The potato takes another 1-2 minutes. The cooking times will vary greatly depending on the grill, thickness and ripeness of the vegetables. Vegetables should be colored yet somewhat crunchy. Remove vegetables to the shallow dish in which they were seasoned. Allow the garlic to cool before removing skin.

## TO PREPARE THE SAUCE:

Juice several carrots to obtain $1/2$ cup of fresh juice. Pour into a small saucepan, place over high heat, and bring to a boil. Reduce the carrot juice by half and remove from heat. Season with salt and pepper.

Taste and adjust seasonings. Set aside and allow to cool.

## TO ASSEMBLE THE SALAD:

Toss the salad greens with $1/4$ of the vinaigrette. Place the salad greens in the center of a large plate. Place the grilled vegetables over and around the salad greens. Pour the remaining vinaigrette over the vegetables. Pour $1/2$ of the sauce around the vegetables on each plate. Garnish with herbs and a few turns of the peppermill just before serving.

*Variation:* Use seasonal vegetables, herbs, or salad to taste.

All the elements are served at room temperature. The sauce may be slightly warm, if desired.

Roast the vegetables in the oven, rather than grilling.

# Salmon Rillettes

*Rillettes are traditionally made with meat, usually pork but also rabbit, goose, or game that is slowly cooked and then shredded along with some fat. It is then usually packed into small ramekins or a terrine mold. This light seafood version is sure to please.*

> 1 cup Aromatic Broth (page 237)
> 5 ounces salmon fillet
> 2½ ounces smoked salmon
> 6 tablespoons softened lightly salted butter
> 2 teaspoons olive oil
> 1 tablespoon lemon juice
> 1 teaspoon lemon peel
> 2 tablespoons heavy whipping cream
> 1 tablespoon chopped dill
> ¼ teaspoon sea salt
> Pinch of freshly ground pepper

Prepare aromatic broth. Bring aromatic broth to boil and poach salmon for 8 minutes or until cooked. Remove salmon from aromatic broth, drain well, and chill thoroughly.

Peel a lemon to obtain 1 teaspoon of peel. Press the lemon to obtain 1 tablespoon of juice. Bring a small pot of water to a boil and blanch lemon peel for approximately 5 minutes. Strain, cool, and finely chop the lemon peel. Reserve.

Cut smoked salmon into small dice and place in food processor with butter, olive oil, lemon juice, chopped lemon peel, dill, and heavy cream.

Process until well mixed, about 30 seconds.

Flake the cooled poached salmon into a mixing bowl and combine with the contents of the food processor. Mix lightly with the aid of a rubber spatula to keep a coarse texture.

Add the seasonings to taste.

Place the rillettes in a terrine or mold and refrigerate. Allow to stand at room temperature for 15 minutes before serving.

*Variation:* Substitute tarragon for the dill.

# Marinated Dill Salmon

*Our version of Gravlax, the Swedish specialty of raw salmon cured in a salt-sugar-dill mixture, is best served in paper-thin slices with sour cream spiked with vodka.*

THE SALMON:

    1 2½-3 pound salmon fillet (skin on)
    ½ cup evaporated cane juice or sugar
    ½ cup sea salt
    2 tablespoons cracked peppercorns
    2 tablespoons cracked coriander seeds
    4-5 bunches dill
    1 8-inch x 10-inch x 4-inch glass or stainless steel container
    1 7-inch x 9-inch lid
    1 8-ounce weight, such as canned food or plastic-covered stone

THE SAUCE:

    4 tablespoons sour cream
    1 teaspoon finely chopped chives
    1 teaspoon vodka
    Sea salt
    Freshly ground pepper

## TO PREPARE THE SALMON:

Combine the salt, sugar, pepper, and coriander and mix thoroughly.

Wash the dill and remove the large stems.

Trim and remove the pin bones from the salmon fillet.

Cut the fillet in half.

Cover the bottom of the container with ¼ of the mixture and 1 bunch of the dill.

Coat each half of the salmon fillet with ¼ of the mixture (flesh side).

Place 1 piece of the coated salmon, skin side down, in the prepared container. Cover with 2 bunches of dill and invert the remaining piece of salmon (flesh side down) onto the dill.

Cover the skin side of the salmon with the remaining mixture and dill. Cover with a sheet of wax paper and place the lid on top. Place the weight on the lid and cover the container with plastic wrap.

Refrigerate and turn salmon every 24 hours. Allow 3-4 days to cure.

*TO PREPARE THE SAUCE:*

Combine all the ingredients in a small bowl and whisk thoroughly. Taste and adjust seasonings.

*TO SERVE:*

Remove salmon from brine and scrape or wipe off pepper and seeds. Slice thinly and serve with lemon wedges, sour cream sauce, and toasted country bread.

*Variation:* Serve with Herb Mayonnaise (page 100).

# Lobster and Asparagus Salad

*Erotic references about asparagus can be traced to ancient Greek and Roman texts. Culpepper's Complete Herbal, a seventeenth century work, states that asparagus "stirreth up bodily lust in man or woman."*

THE LOBSTER:

> 1 1¼ pound lobster

THE VANILLA VINAIGRETTE:

> 2 vanilla beans
> ⅓ cup champagne or white wine vinegar
> ⅓ cup vegetable oil
> ½ teaspoon finely minced shallots
> Sea salt
> Freshly ground pepper
> Pinch of evaporated cane juice or sugar (optional)

THE SALAD:

> 8-10 stalks of lightly steamed asparagus
> 2 ounces (2 cups) mesclun salad, mixed baby lettuce

## TO PREPARE THE ASPARAGUS AND LOBSTER:

Fill a pot fitted with a steamer top with salted water and bring to a boil. Steam the asparagus to *al dente*, remove, and allow to cool. Place the lobster in the steamer, cover, and cook for approximately 8-10 minutes until the lobster is just cooked through. Remove and allow to cool.

Crack the claws to remove the meat. Split the lobster tail down the center and remove the meat. Reserve with the lobster claws.

## TO PREPARE THE VINAIGRETTE:

Split the vanilla bean in half lengthwise and scrape the seeds from the insides of the pod. Combine the split beans, vanilla seeds, and vinegar in a small saucepan and bring to a boil. Immediately remove pan from heat and allow to steep for 5 minutes. Remove the split beans from the pan.

Combine the oil and shallots in a small mixing bowl and whisk in the vinegar from the saucepan. Scrape the pan with a rubber spatula to retrieve all of the vanilla seeds.

Season with sea salt, freshly ground pepper, and a pinch of sweetener, if desired. The sweetener enhances the flavor of the vanilla.

## TO ASSEMBLE THE SALAD:

Divide the well-drained and cooled asparagus between two serving plates. Place the washed and well-drained salad in a mixing bowl, add $1/2$ of the vinaigrette, and toss. Divide the salad between the two servings of asparagus. Cover the stems but leave the asparagus tips exposed.

Divide the lobster and claws between the two salads, placing them on top of the salad greens.

Spoon the remaining vinaigrette over the lobster and asparagus tips.

Serve at once.

*Hint*: A neutral vegetable oil is preferred for the taste, as a scented oil such as extra virgin olive oil tends to overwhelm the vanilla. A cold pressed oil is preferred for your health. Health and taste do occasionally conflict.

# Marinated Rockfish

*This version of Seviche, marinated fish that is "cooked" in a delicious combination of ingredients, is a light and lusty dish.*

THE ROCKFISH:

  4-5 ounces sushi-grade rockfish fillet
  Level $^1/_2$ teaspoon sea salt
  Freshly ground pepper
  $^1/_2$ teaspoon ground anise seed
  $^1/_3$ teaspoon ground coriander

THE VINAIGRETTE:

  $^1/_2$ teaspoon Dijon-style mustard
  1 tablespoon extra virgin olive oil
  3 tablespoons lemon juice
  Pinch of cayenne pepper
  1 bunch of watercress

## TO PREPARE THE FISH:

Trim away any skin or blood line from the fillet. Thinly slice the fillet with a very sharp knife. Divide the slices between two serving plates. Season with salt, pepper, and the ground seeds.

Prepare a vinaigrette with the remaining ingredients. Spoon the vinaigrette over the prepared fish. Cover, refrigerate, and allow to marinate for at least 1 hour for rare and about 3 hours for "cooked through."

## TO SERVE:

Clean, drain, and trim the watercress and place in a salad bowl. Remove the plates of fish from the refrigerator. Pour off the excess vinaigrette over the watercress and toss to season. Divide the seasoned watercress over the marinated fish.

Season the fish and salad with a few turns of the peppermill and serve.

*Variation:* Substitute other fish, such as red snapper, flounder, grouper, etc.

# Beef Carpaccio

*A delightful combination of ingredients, this will prove that you have both taste and style. A certain amount of raw food in the diet is essential. Cooking food past 112 degrees deactivates important enzymes.*

THE BEEF:

> 6-8 ounces center cut beef tenderloin
> Freshly ground pepper
> 1 teaspoon finely chopped tarragon

THE SAUCE:

> $\frac{1}{3}$ cup Mayonnaise (made with olive oil) (page 245)
> 1 teaspoon Dijon-style mustard
> $\frac{1}{2}$ teaspoon lemon juice
> $\frac{1}{3}$ teaspoon finely chopped tarragon
> Pinch of cayenne pepper
> Sea salt
> Freshly ground pepper

THE GARNISH:

> 2-3 ounces extra-sharp cheddar, parmesan, or gruyère
> 1 teaspoon capers, drained
> Daikon radish sprouts

Trim any fat and/or silver skin from the beef tenderloin. Season the beef with pepper and chopped tarragon. Wrap the seasoned tenderloin in plastic wrap, forming a cylindrical shape. Place the beef in the freezer for at least 2 hours to firm.

The paper-thin slices of beef are possible only when the meat is chilled to an almost frozen state.

Remove the beef from the freezer, unwrap, and slice as thinly as possible with a very sharp knife or meat slicer. Allow at least 15 minutes before serving for beef to defrost.

Arrange slices in concentric circles on each serving plate. May be prepared ahead, covered, and refrigerated until time to serve.

## TO PREPARE THE SAUCE:

Prepare the sauce by combining all the ingredients in a small bowl and whisking thoroughly. Taste and adjust seasonings.

## TO SERVE:

Using a plastic squeeze bottle, make a criss-cross pattern with the sauce over the beef and sides of the plate, or spoon the sauce around the edges of the plate.

Slice the cheese in a julienne and spread over the beef. If using parmesan, shave over the beef. Scatter the capers over the beef.

Place a bunch of sprouts in the center of the plate.

Season with sea salt and freshly ground pepper.

*Variation:* Use extra virgin olive oil instead of the sauce.

# Marinated Beef Salad

*This beef adaptation of seviche is delicious and nutritious.*

THE VINAIGRETTE:

>   1 large ripe tomato
>   $\frac{1}{2}$ cup extra virgin olive oil
>   1$\frac{1}{2}$ tablespoons balsamic vinegar
>   $\frac{1}{2}$ teaspoon Dijon-style mustard
>   1 teaspoon finely chopped parsley
>   2 tablespoons diced carrot
>   2 tablespoons diced celery root (substitute celery)

THE BEEF:

>   8-10 ounces beef tenderloin

THE GARNISH:

>   Bunch spicy sprouts

## TO PREPARE THE TOMATO VINAIGRETTE:

Bring a quart of water to a boil. Add the tomato to the pot of boiling water for about 20 seconds. Lift the tomato out of the boiling water with a slotted spoon and drop into a bowl of ice water. Cool the tomato a few moments and remove from the cold water.

Peel off the skin and remove the stem. Slice the tomato in half and place in a colander set over a bowl. Press the tomato halves to force out the juice and seeds. Use in another recipe.

Dice tomato and place in a medium mixing bowl.

Combine all the ingredients except the oil in a bowl and beat together with a wire whisk until well blended. Gradually pour in the oil, whisking constantly. Taste and adjust seasonings.

## TO PREPARE THE BEEF:

Trim away any fat and silver skin from the beef tenderloin.

Wrap the beef in plastic film and place in freezer for about 15 minutes to facilitate slicing.

Remove the beef tenderloin from the freezer, thinly slice, and lightly salt and pepper the beef. Combine the prepared beef with the vinaigrette, tossing well.

Cover the bowl with plastic film and refrigerate for 5-6 hours or overnight before serving to allow the beef to marinate.

## TO SERVE:

Divide the marinated beef between two serving plates and season with a few turns of the peppermill.

Garnish the plates with the spicy sprouts and serve.

*Variation:* Divide the marinated beef over a bed of lettuce.

# My Favorite Chef Salad

*My favorite late night snack after a day of cooking in a hot kitchen.*

THE VINAIGRETTE:

>    1 small garlic clove, chopped
>    ½ teaspoon Dijon-style mustard
>    ½ teaspoon fresh chopped tarragon or parsley
>    3 teaspoons vinegar
>    3 tablespoons extra virgin olive oil
>    Sea salt
>    Freshly ground pepper

*FOR THE SALAD:*

>    4 ounces beef tenderloin or flank steak
>    2 ounces raw milk cheese (gruyère or cheddar)
>    2 ounces salad greens (small handful)
>    2 tablespoons each julienne carrot, beets, and celery
>       (substitute celery root)
>    4 raw asparagus
>    1 tablespoon of bean or spicy sprouts

*TO PREPARE THE VINAIGRETTE:*

Combine all the ingredients, except the oil, in a small bowl and beat together with a whisk until they are well blended. Gradually beat in the oil. Taste and adjust seasonings.

*TO PREPARE THE SALAD:*

Place the beef in the freezer for 10-15 minutes to facilitate slicing.

While the beef is chilling, prepare the salads.

Wash and thoroughly drain the salad greens. Divide the prepared greens between two serving plates.

Wash, peel, and julienne the vegetables and scatter over the salad greens.

Julienne the cheese and set aside.

*Soft Boiled Eggs with*
*Salmon Roe (page 7)*

*Apple and Roquefort Tart (page 12)*

*Potato Rosti with Currant-Glazed Peaches (page 13)*

*Shrimp with Garlic and Herb Butter (page 32)*

*Poached Halibut with Sea Vegetables (page 36)*

*Chicken in Champagne Sauce (page 45)*

*Lobster and Asparagus Salad* (page 73)

*Citrus Salad with Ginger (page 87)*

*Frozen Raspberry Soufflés (page 89)*

*Crabmeat in a Potato Crust (page 98)*

Cold Salmon with a Sesame Crust (page 100)

Châteaubriand of Tuna (page 106)

Remove the beef from the freezer and thinly slice. Divide the beef and then the prepared cheese and scatter over the prepared vegetables and salad greens.

Place a small bunch of sprouts on top of the cheese.

Pepper the salads and pour the vinaigrette over the 2 salads.

Serve at once.

*Hint:* Plate the salads, cover with plastic wrap, and refrigerate ahead of time. Pour the vinaigrette over just prior to serving.

# Papa's Alsatian Potato Salad

*Mustard, like other warming spices, has long been touted as a sexual stimulant.*

2 medium Russet potatoes
2 thick sliced strips of bacon
2 tablespoons minced white or red onions
1 tablespoon minced chives or green onions
$1/4$ teaspoon minced garlic
1 teaspoon dry mustard or 2 heaping teaspoons Dijon mustard
$1/2$ teaspoon red wine vinegar
$1/3$ cup Vinaigrette (page 245)
Sea salt
Freshly ground pepper

Place potatoes in a pan and cover with cold water; add 1 teaspoon of salt and bring to a boil. Cook the potatoes for approximately 15 minutes, until just slightly firm when pierced with a fork. Drain potatoes and cover with cold water. Once cool to the touch, peel the potatoes; split them lengthwise and thickly slice ($1/8$-inch thick).

Place sliced potatoes in a large mixing bowl.

Dice the bacon and sauté until slightly crisp. Pour the hot bacon, grease and all (that's the best part and the secret of Papa's recipe) onto the potatoes. Add the remaining ingredients and toss gently using a rubber spatula. Salt and pepper to taste.

# Lentil Salad

*This member of the pea family is rich in iron, copper, and phosphorus. This salad will become one of your lover's favorites.*

THE LENTILS:

> ¹/₂ pound lentils
> ¹/₂ medium carrot
> ¹/₂ medium onion
> ¹/₂ stalk of celery
> 2 cloves
> 1 bay leaf

THE SALAD:

> 1 thick strip of bacon (1 ounce)
> 1 tablespoon chopped onion
> 1 tablespoon diced tomato
> ¹/₃ cup dry white wine
> ¹/₄ teaspoon minced garlic
> Sea salt
> freshly ground pepper
> ¹/₄ cup Vinaigrette (page 245)

## TO COOK THE LENTILS:

Wash the lentils. Place 2 cups of cold water in a medium saucepan. Add the whole piece of carrot, celery stalk, onion, cloves, and bay leaves. Season with salt and pepper. Bring to a boil and cook until the vegetables are soft, approximately 15-20 minutes. Remove the vegetables from the water, set aside and allow to cool. Add the lentils to the broth and return to a boil. Cook for 18-20 minutes or until the lentils are slightly firm. Drain the lentils in a colander set over a bowl to capture the liquid.

## TO PREPARE THE SALAD:

Dice the cooled carrot, celery, and onion.

Dice the bacon and sauté in a large saucepan until nicely browned. Add the minced onion and sauté for 1 minute, being careful not to burn the onion. Carefully pour in the white wine and reduce by half. Add $1/2$ the cooking liquid, the diced tomato, reserved vegetables, and minced garlic. Bring to a boil, adjust seasoning, and add the cooked lentils. Cool.

Add about $1/4$ cup of vinaigrette to the cooled lentils. Taste and adjust seasonings, adding more vinaigrette, if necessary.

*Hint:* May be prepared a day ahead.

# Strawberry and Rhubarb Salad

*The word rhubarb comes from the Latin rha barbarum, barbarian rhubarb. The plant came from outside the empire, and hence, the land of the barbarians. Chinese folk medicine recommends rhubarb to stimulate passion.*

> 5-6 stalks of rhubarb (6-8 ounces)
> $1/3$ cup evaporated cane juice or sugar
> $1/2$ cup water
> 1 tablespoon lemon juice
> $1/2$ vanilla bean
> 8 large strawberries
> 12 mint leaves

### TO PREPARE THE RHUBARB:

Trim the ends and lightly peel the outermost filaments of the stalks. Split the prepared stalks down the center lengthwise and cut into $1/4$-$1/2$-inch dice. Approximately 1 cup should remain. Place the diced rhubarb in a small bowl and mix thoroughly with the sweetener. Cover and refrigerate overnight.

The following day, use a rubber spatula to scrape the prepared rhubarb into a strainer set over a bowl to collect the juice. Allow the rhubarb to drain for 5 minutes, tossing occasionally. Place the rhubarb back into the bowl and reserve.

### TO PREPARE THE SYRUP:

Transfer the strained juice to a small saucepan and add the water, split vanilla bean, lemon juice, and 8 mint leaves. Place over high heat and bring to a boil, reduce heat, and simmer about 4 minutes. Approximately $1/3$ cup should remain. Remove from heat and strain the hot syrup over the reserved rhubarb. Chill.

### TO SERVE:

Divide the prepared rhubarb between two serving bowls. Wash, stem, and slice the strawberries and place around the edges of the bowls. Garnish with the 4 reserved mint leaves.

# Blood Orange Salad

*Blood oranges have dark red pulp and the skin may be veined with dark red. They are available from December to April. The juice makes one of our most appreciated sorbets at the restaurant.*

> 6 blood oranges
> ¹/₂ cup honey
> ¹/₂ cup raspberries
> 2 tablespoons Grand Marnier or orange liqueur
> 1 tablespoon sliced raw almonds or sesame seeds

Using a vegetable peeler, peel 2 of the oranges, being careful to remove only the outer skin, avoiding the bitter inner skin. Press the 2 blood oranges to obtain the juice.

Cut the peel into a thin julienne.

Bring 1 cup of water to a boil over high heat, add the julienne, and blanch for 1 minute. Drain the blood orange julienne.

Using a sharp knife, cut away the skin of the remaining 4 oranges, removing all of the skin.

Thinly slice the oranges cross-wise over a plate to recover any juice.

Divide the orange slices between two shallow serving bowls.

Place the reserved orange juice and raspberries in a small saucepan and bring to a boil. Whisk thoroughly to crush the raspberries, and reduce the liquid by half. Strain the liquid into a bowl to remove the raspberry seeds. Add the honey to the warm liquid and whisk thoroughly to dissolve. Add the reserved julienne and Grand Marnier to the prepared syrup.

Divide the syrup between the 2 serving bowls of oranges.

Cover the bowls and refrigerate for at least ¹/₂ hour before serving.

Scatter slivered almonds over the oranges just before serving.

*Hint:* Use raw unfiltered honey for optimal nutritional benefits and add after cooking to retain the active enzymes.

*Variation:* Prepare with any orange.

# Citrus Salad with Ginger

*Ginger is credited with aiding digestion, improving circulation, and even protecting against motion sickness.*

    2 oranges
    2 small grapefruit
    1 banana
    1 kiwi
    1 teaspoon finely chopped fresh ginger
    2 tablespoons evaporated cane juice or sugar

Using a sharp knife, cut away the outer rind and white membrane of both the oranges and grapefruits. Section the citrus by cutting along the longitudinal membranes. Peel and slice banana and kiwi into $1/4$ inch rounds.

Place the prepared fruit in a bowl. Add the ginger and sweetener.

Allow to marinate in the refrigerator for at least $1/2$ hour before serving.

Garnish with mint leaves.

*Variation:* Sweeten with honey.

# Spiced Strawberries

*The dried unripe berry of a tree grown in Jamaica and Indonesia, Allspice has an aromatic flavor that blends cloves, cinnamon, and nutmeg.*

$\frac{1}{3}$ cup water
2 tablespoons evaporated cane juice or sugar
$\frac{1}{2}$ vanilla bean, split or 1 teaspoon vanilla extract
1 whole clove
4 allspice berries, crushed
Pinch of nutmeg
$\frac{1}{3}$ cup sweet late harvest wine
1 pint strawberries
Mint leaves

Place the water, evaporated cane juice, vanilla bean, clove, allspice, and nutmeg in a small saucepan over high heat and bring to a boil.

Reduce heat and simmer uncovered for 5 minutes. Remove from heat and allow to cool. If using vanilla extract, add it now.

Wash and cap the strawberries. Drain well and place in a small bowl.

Mix the sweet wine into the syrup, taste and adjust seasonings, and strain over the strawberries. Allow strawberries to marinate 1 hour in the refrigerator before serving.

Garnish with mint leaves before serving.

# Frozen Raspberry Soufflés

*Frozen soufflés are a perfect make-ahead warm weather dessert. The raspberry fruit brandy adds a deeper, more concentrated raspberry flavor to the soufflé. Parchment paper is used to extend the sides and act as a collar. Your guest is bound to be pleased by the rich cool taste.*

## THE SOUFFLÉS:

>    1 pint raspberries
>    1$\frac{1}{2}$ tablespoons honey
>    1 whole egg
>    1 cup heavy whipping cream
>    2 teaspoons *Framboise* (raspberry brandy)

## THE MOLDS:

>    2 6-ounce soufflé ramekins
>    2 12 x 3$\frac{1}{2}$-inch strips of parchment paper
>    Butter

## TO MAKE THE SOUFFLÉS:

Clean and remove any stems from the raspberries. Reserve 20 nice berries for later use. Purée the raspberries in a food processor and strain to remove the seeds. Approximately $\frac{2}{3}$ cup of purée should remain.

Break the egg into a glass or stainless steel bowl or double boiler. Add the honey and whisk thoroughly.

Place the bowl over a pan of hot, simmering water or double boiler. Beat continuously, using the whisk to scrape the egg from the sides and bottom of the bowl. Cook for approximately 1 minute or until the egg thickens slightly. Add the raspberry brandy to the purée and stir into the egg and honey mixture.

Set the bowl aside.

Whip the heavy cream and fold into the egg and raspberry mixture. Stir in all but 2 of the reserved whole raspberries. Refrigerate.

## TO ASSEMBLE THE SOUFFLÉS:

Butter the strips of parchment paper. Form a collar around each mold, buttered side in, with the strip of parchment and secure with tape.

Fill the mold to the top of the collar with the mixture and freeze for at least 6 hours or overnight.

## TO SERVE:

Remove the collar and top the soufflés with the reserved raspberries. Allow to stand at room temperature for about 15 minutes before serving.

# Two's Company

It's a typical Tuesday night, but of course, every night with your beloved is joyous. When you are in love, no day is ordinary.

Working too hard lately? Or maybe you need to rekindle the flame?

With a little planning and effort, even an uneventful evening may turn amorous.

These dishes are straightforward, not overly costly, and require relatively modest preparation time.

Pick your evening, spend a little of your spare time shopping for just the right ingredients, and set aside some prep time; then dazzle your guest with your culinary magic.

Some of these recipes can be made over the weekend and reheated— just add some cool jazz and you can't miss.

# Suggested Menus

♦♦♦

Oyster and Apple Cider Soup
Rockfish with Vermouth Sauce
Warm Apple Tarts

Oysters with Horseradish Sauce
Lamb Chops with Barley
Beer Ice Cream

Mushroom Crêpes
Châteaubriand of Tuna
Warm Chocolate Tart

Mussel Soup
Coffee-Marinated Veal Chops
Snow Eggs

Crabmeat in a Potato Crust
Veal Scallopini with Gruyère Cheese
Quince Crème Brûlée

# Oyster and Apple Cider Soup

*We often give the gift of sweets or flowers to the ones we love. In the ancient world, apples served the same purpose. In Norse mythology, the gods ate apples to restore youthful vigor. An apple a day will make your lover stay. This unique soup is sure to heat up the evening*

> 10 oysters: Malpeque, Wellfleet, etc.
> $2/_3$ cup fresh apple cider
> $1/_2$ teaspoon apple cider vinegar
> $1/_3$ cup finely diced apple, Granny Smith or Ginger Gold
> 1 tablespoon finely chopped chives
> 1 tablespoon finely minced shallots
> Sea salt
> Freshly ground pepper

Shuck the oysters, reserving the oyster liquor.

Combine the oyster liquor and apple cider vinegar with the apple cider. Season with salt and pepper.

Peel and core the apple; about $1/_2$ apple makes $1/_3$ cup, and finely dice. Combine with the cider mixture.

Divide the seasoned apple cider between two shallow serving bowls. Divide the oysters between the two bowls. Lightly pepper the oysters and sprinkle each with equal parts of the minced shallots and minced chives.

Serve immediately.

*Variation:* Substitute freshly pressed apple juice for the cider. Add $1/_2$ teaspoon lemon juice to maintain color.

# Mussel Soup

*Ancient Welsh warriors believed that leeks gave them strength and went into battle wearing only a garland of leeks around their necks. Buy so called "rope" mussels. They are suspended off the ocean bottom in sacks and for the most part are much cleaner outside with less internal grit.*

### THE MUSSELS:

>  1 pound whole mussels
>  2 cups dry white wine
>  1 tablespoon finely minced shallots
>  Pinch of garlic
>  Sprig of fresh thyme and/or parsley
>  1 bay leaf
>  Sea salt
>  Freshly ground pepper

### THE SOUP:

>  4 tablespoons butter
>  2 tablespoons finely chopped onion
>  2 tablespoons finely chopped carrot
>  2 tablespoons finely chopped leek (white only)
>  2 tablespoons flour
>  Pinch of saffron
>  $\frac{1}{2}$ cup heavy whipping cream

## TO PREPARE THE MUSSELS:

Clean the mussels individually under cold running water, scraping off any clinging barnacles or "beards." Discard any that do not shut tightly or any unusually heavy ones, indicating internal grit.

Place the white wine, shallots, garlic, bay leaf, thyme, pinch of salt, and pepper in a large saucepan. Bring to a boil over high heat, cover and cook 2-3 minutes. Add the cleaned mussels, cover and cook for several minutes, tossing once or twice, until the mussels are all open. Remove from heat and reserve.

## TO PREPARE THE SOUP:

In another saucepan, melt 2 tablespoons of butter and add the chopped onion, carrot, and leek. Cook on low heat for 3-4 minutes until vegetables are tender, being careful not to brown them. Pour all of the liquid from the pan of mussels into the pan containing the cooked vegetables. Place over high heat and bring to a boil. Lower heat and boil gently for about 10 minutes.

Soften the remaining 2 tablespoons of butter and combine with the 2 tablespoons of flour using a fork. Whisk the flour/butter into the boiling liquid, add the saffron, and simmer for another 10 minutes. Strain the soup into another saucepan, add the heavy cream and adjust seasonings.

## TO SERVE:

Shell the mussels and divide between warm soup bowls, add soup and serve.

# Oysters with Horseradish Sauce

*Casanova, referring to oysters in his voluminous memoirs, confesses that to eat "so delicate a morsel must be a sin in itself."*

> 10-12 Bluepoint oysters
> 1 cup heavy whipping cream
> 1 teaspoon grated horseradish
> Sea salt
> Freshly ground pepper.

Open the oysters and place the oysters on the half shell in a plate to collect any oyster liquor.

Combine the heavy cream and oyster liquor in a small saucepan. Bring to a boil over high flame and continue to boil for 3-4 minutes to reduce volume by half. Whisk in the grated horseradish and bring up to a boil again. Remove from heat and season with salt, pepper, and more horseradish, if desired. Keep warm.

*Preheat the broiler.*

Place each oyster on the half shell on a special oyster baking dish or on a bed of rock salt to hold them level. Place the oysters under the boiler for about 1 minute or until just warm, being careful not to overcook. Coat each oyster with approximately 1 teaspoon of the warm sauce and serve immediately.

*Variation:* use any fresh local oysters such as Belon, Moonstone, Winter Point, etc.

# Mushroom Crêpes

*Crêpes are essentially very thin pancakes and may be either sweet or savory. The word comes from the Latin, Crispus, meaning curly or wavy. Traditionally crêpes were served to celebrate renewal, good fortune, and future happiness.*

THE SAVORY CRÊPE BATTER:

> 4 whole eggs
> 1 1/2 cups half and half
> 7 ounces flour
> 1/4 teaspoon nutmeg
> 2 tablespoons brown butter
> 1 teaspoon finely chopped chives or parsley
> Sea salt
> Freshly ground pepper

THE CRÊPES:

> Butter
> Oil
> 1/2 cup *Duxelles* (page 246)

Beat the eggs in a glass or stainless steel bowl. Whisk in the half and half. While whisking, gradually add the flour. Add seasonings and herbs. Brown the 2 tablespoons of butter in a small pan and add to the mixture.

In a small 6-7 inch skillet or non-stick pan, melt 1/2 teaspoon of butter with a few drops of oil. When the butter begins to brown, add approximately 1 ounce of batter, enough to make a thin crêpe; be careful to evenly coat the entire bottom of the pan. Cook a few moments until the batter is set and flip crêpe to brown the other side. Allow to cool on a rack before stacking.

Heat the *duxelles*, taste, and adjust seasonings. Place a crêpe on a warm plate and spoon 2 tablespoons of the hot *duxelles* into the center of the crêpe. Fold the crêpe over to form a half circle. Serve 2 crêpes per person.

*Hint:* Store the remaining crêpes in freezer for later use.

# Crabmeat in a Potato Crust

*Queen Marie Antoinette of France was known to wear potato blossoms in her hair. It is not certain whether her hair was adorned with them when she lost her head. With most of its nutrients found just under the skin, potatoes provide vitamins C and B-complex, as well as potassium, calcium, and iron. Peppers are also rich in vitamin C, calcium, and potassium. Red peppers are richer in these than green ones.*

### THE CRAB:

> 6 ounces jumbo lump crabmeat
> 2 tablespoons butter or olive oil
> 1 teaspoon finely minced shallots
> 1/2 teaspoon finely chopped dill
> 1/2 teaspoon lemon juice
> Sea salt
> Freshly ground pepper

### THE CRUST:

> 1 large Russet potato
> 1/3 cup extra virgin olive oil
> Sea salt
> Freshly ground pepper
> 2 6-ounce ramekins, approximately 3-inch diameter by 2-inches high

### THE PEPPER COULIS:

> 1 large red or yellow bell pepper
> 1/2 teaspoon olive oil (approximately)
> Sea salt
> Freshly ground pepper

## TO PREPARE THE CRABMEAT:

Carefully remove any pieces of shell from the crabmeat. Melt the 2 tablespoons of butter in a small sauté pan. When the butter begins to brown, add the shallots, cook a few seconds, and then add the crabmeat and a pinch of salt and pepper. Toss gently and add the dill and lemon juice. Set aside and cool.

## TO PREPARE THE POTATO CRUST:

*Preheat the oven to 375 degrees*

Lightly coat the bottom of cookie sheet with the olive oil.

Wash and peel the potato. Using a very sharp knife or vegetable slicer, cut 8-10 paper-thin lengthwise slices of potato.

Place the slices of potato on the prepared baking sheet.

Brush the slices of potato with olive oil.

Bake in the preheated oven for approximately 3-4 minutes until the slices are translucent.

Carefully transfer, with a spatula, the blanched potato slices onto paper towels to remove excess oil. Season with salt and set aside.

*Preheat oven to 400 degrees.*

Brush the 2 ramekins with olive oil and line with 4-5 of the blanched potato slices. Slices must overlap and extend over the edge of the molds.

Fill each prepared mold with the seasoned crabmeat and fold the edges of the blanched potato slices back over the crabmeat to cover completely.

Bake the prepared ramekins for 10 minutes. Remove from oven and invert the ramekins onto a small sheet pan coated with olive oil. Return to oven and bake another 8-10 minutes until golden brown.

## TO PREPARE THE COULIS:

Wipe the bell pepper clean. Coat lightly with oil and blacken the skin all around over an open flame.

Dip pepper in a small container of cold water to loosen the skin. Peel off the skin.

Cut the prepared pepper in half and remove stem and seeds.

Place pepper in a blender or food processor and purée.

Season with salt and pepper and refrigerate.

## TO SERVE:

Serve with the bell pepper coulis and garnish with spicy sprouts.

# Cold Salmon with Black Sesame Crust and Herb Mayonnaise

*A homemade mayonnaise prepared with free range eggs, extra virgin olive oil, and fresh herbs is delicious and nutritious.*

THE HERB MAYONNAISE:

> ¹/₂ cup Mayonnaise (page 245)
> 2 teaspoons finely chopped watercress
> 1 tablespoon finely chopped parsley
> 1 small hard-boiled egg, chopped
> ¹/₂ teaspoon Dijon-sytle mustard
> ¹/₂ teaspoon lemon juice
> ¹/₂ teaspoon finely minced onion
> ¹/₂ teaspoon finely chopped chives
> 1 teaspoon finely chopped fresh tarragon
> ¹/₂ teaspoon finely chopped capers
> Sea salt
> Pinch of freshly ground pepper
> Pinch of cayenne pepper

THE SALMON:

> 1 recipe Aromatic Broth (page 237)
> 2 ounces black sesame seeds
> 10 ounces skinless salmon fillet
> Butter
> Sea salt
> Freshly ground pepper

## TO PREPARE THE MAYONNAISE SAUCE:

Place the mayonnaise in a small mixing bowl.

Put the parsley and watercress in a piece of clean cheesecloth, twist the ends together to close, and squeeze the juice from the herbs into the mayonnaise.

Add the remaining ingredients, including the watercress and parsley. Blend thoroughly. Taste and adjust the seasonings. Chill until ready to serve.

## TO PREPARE THE SALMON:

*Preheat oven to 450 degrees*

Cut the salmon into 2 equal fillets. Season with salt and pepper and press the sesame seeds into 1 side of each filet to form a crust. Place fillets in a buttered baking pan and add approximately 1 cup of the Aromatic Broth. The broth should just cover the bottom of the pan to a depth of $1/4$ so as not to rinse away the sesame seeds. Bring to a boil on top of the stove and place in a pre-heated 425-degree oven for approximately 7 minutes or until the fish is just cooked through. Remove from the oven and allow to cool right in the cooking pan. Cover and refrigerate.

## TO SERVE:

Place the cooled salmon on two chilled plates and garnish with the mayonnaise. Serve with a mixed salad, if desired.

# Roasted Rockfish

*"Rockfish" is the Chesapeake Bay colloquialism for the striped bass. It is greatly prized and very delicious! Strut your culinary stuff by presenting the roasted fish to your guest right out of the oven. Then transfer and filet the fish at the table.*

### THE VEGETABLES:

    1 small turnip
    1 medium potato
    1 medium carrot
    4-6 white pearl onions
    1 white of leek
    1 stalk of celery

### THE FISH:

    1 whole 2 pound rockfish
    2 tablespoons butter
    1 teaspoon oil
    Sea salt
    Freshly ground pepper
    ¾ cup Chicken Sauce (page 45)

## *TO PREPARE THE VEGETABLES:*

Peel the turnip and potato. Cut each in half and cut each half into 4 wedges.

Peel the carrot, split down the middle, and cut each half into 4 lengths.

Peel the pearl onions.

Split and thoroughly wash the leek. Cut the white of the leek into four.

Trim and wash the celery and cut four 2-inch sections.

Steam the vegetables over salted water until just cooked through and crisp, *al dente*.

Approximate cooking times:  leeks and celery - 7 minutes.
                          turnips and carrots - 8 minutes.
                          potatoes and onions - 11 minutes.

Cooking time will vary depending on the size of the vegetables. Reserve steamed vegetables.

The vegetables may be prepared ahead of time.

## TO PREPARE THE FISH:

*Preheat oven to 450 degrees.*

Scale fish, gut and rinse, leaving the fish whole. Season inside and out with sea salt and pepper.

Place butter and oil in a roasting pan just large enough to accommodate the rockfish. Place the roasting pan over high heat. When the butter just begins to brown, place the rockfish in the pan. Cook the fish on the stove top for approximately 2 minutes. Turn the fish over with the aid of a spatula. Place the pan in a heated oven and roast the fish for approximately 8 minutes. Add the chicken stock and prepared vegetables to the roasting pan and cook another 5 minutes until the sauce boils and the fish is just cooked through.

Remove the roasting pan from the oven and present at table.

After presenting the fish right from the oven in the roasting pan, remove the rockfish from the pan and place on a large platter. Filet the fish with the aid of 2 forks and divide onto two warm plates. Divide the vegetables between the two plates and pour some of the Chicken Sauce around the fillets. Serve immediately.

*Variation:* Substitute black bass.

# Alsatian Fish Stew

*This dish, called Matelote in France, is a fish stew made with red or white wine and aromatic flavorings. Matelote made with white wine and local freshwater fish is an Alsatian classic. My version incorporates fresh and saltwater fish as well as shellfish.*

THE SEAFOOD:

> $^1/_4$ pound sea scallops
> $^1/_4$ pound shrimp, peeled and deveined
> $^1/_3$ pound white fish: sea bass, halibut, cod
> $^1/_3$ pound salmon
> 6 mussels
> 6 clams

THE SAUCE:

> 2 tablespoons butter
> 1 tablespoon finely minced shallots
> $^2/_3$ cup Riesling wine
> $^1/_2$ cup Fish Stock (page 235)
> 1 tablespoon each softened butter and all-purpose flour
> $^1/_3$ cup heavy whipping cream
> Sea salt
> Freshly ground pepper

## TO PREPARE THE SEAFOOD:

*Preheat the oven to 375 degrees.*

Skin the fish and cut into small (2-inch x 2-inch) pieces.

Wash the scallops and shrimp in cold water and drain well.

Clean the mussels individually under cold running water, scraping off any clinging barnacles or "beards." Discard any half-open shells or any unusually heavy ones, indicating internal grit. Rinse the clams in cold water.

Smear 2 tablespoons of butter and 1 tablespoon shallots in a small (9-inch by 13-inch) baking pan. Place the sliced fish fillets in the pan in a single layer. Season with salt and pepper and pour $\frac{1}{2}$ cup of wine and $\frac{1}{2}$ cup of fish stock over the fish. Place the pan over direct heat until the liquid begins to boil. Cover the pan with a lid or sheet of foil and set in the preheated oven for approximately 5 minutes until the fish is just cooked through.

## TO PREPARE THE SAUCE:

While the fish is cooking, melt another 2 tablespoons of the butter in a small saucepan over medium heat. Add the remaining 1 tablespoon of shallots and simmer momentarily. Do not let them brown. Add the shrimp and scallops and simmer until the shrimp begin to redden. Add the remaining wine and fish stock. Bring to a boil over high heat and immediately remove the shrimp and scallops with a slotted spoon. Cover the seafood. Add the clams and mussels to the liquid and cook until they open. Remove the clams and mussels from the pan with a slotted spoon.

Combine the cooking liquids from both pans of fish. Reduce the liquid by half.

Blend the 1 tablespoon of softened butter with the flour to make a *beurre manié*. Whisk it into the boiling liquid and boil gently for 5-8 minutes. Whisk occasionally to prevent lumps from forming. Add the heavy cream, boil for 1-2 minutes, and remove from heat. Taste and adjust seasonings.

## TO SERVE:

Divide the fish and seafood into two large warm soup bowls. Coat with the sauce and serve. Garnish with slices of toasted country bread.

# Châteaubriand of Tuna with Baked Tomatoes

*A traditional "Château" is the center cut of the beef tenderloin. The Châteaubriand in this case is the center cut of the loin of tuna. In the Middle Ages, people put Rosemary sprigs under their pillows to keep nightmares away. Thyme under your bed was supposed to ensure a good nights sleep.*

THE FISH:

> 1 16-18 ounce center cut of yellowfin tuna
> 1 teaspoon cracked black peppercorns
> Olive oil
> Sea salt
> ¼ cup Chive Oil (page 244)

THE BAKED TOMATOES:

> 2 ripe medium tomatoes
> Sea salt
> Freshly ground pepper
> Olive oil

THE HERB BREAD CRUMBS:

> 2 tablespoons butter
> 1 teaspoon finely minced garlic
> ½ cup plain bread crumbs
> ½ teaspoon sea salt
> Pinch of freshly ground pepper
> ½ teaspoon of combined ground rosemary, thyme, and bay leaf or
>     *Herbes de Provence*
> 1 tablespoon freshly chopped parsley

## TO PREPARE THE TUNA:

Trim away any silver skin or blood line that covers the tuna. Season the tuna with the cracked peppercorns, coat with olive oil, and marinate overnight in the refrigerator.

*Preheat the grill.*

Remove the tuna from the marinade. Allow a thin coating of the marinade to remain on the fish. Season with the salt and grill, allowing approximately 6-8 minutes per side for medium rare.

## TO PREPARE THE HERB BREAD CRUMBS:

Melt butter in a small saucepan. Add the garlic and cook 5 seconds. Immedlately mix in the bread crumbs, salt, pepper, spices, and parsley. Thoroughly blend in the ingredients with a large spoon and remove from the heat.

## TO PREPARE THE TOMATOES:

*Preheat oven to 400 degrees*

Wash and dry the tomatoes. Remove the stems with a small knife and cut each tomato in half, crosswise. Brush with a little olive oil, season with salt and pepper, and place in a baking pan. Bake the tomatoes approximately 6-8 minutes, only enough to heat them thoroughly. Cooking time will vary, depending upon the ripeness of the tomatoes. Remove from oven.

*Increase oven temperature to broil.*

When ready to serve the tomatoes, generously sprinkle each half with Herb Bread Crumbs. Brown lightly under the broiler and serve.

## TO SERVE:

Slice the tuna on a slant into four pieces and arrange down the center of a platter. Garnish with the baked tomatoes and with other assorted grilled or roasted vegetables, such as small whole onions, squash, or potatoes. Decorate with squash blossoms, if available.

Serve with the chive oil.

*Variation:* Sear the tuna on all sides in a skillet and bake in an oven preheated to 425 degrees for about 12 minutes for medium rare.

# Bouillabaisse

*Raymond Oliver, author of* Gastronomy of France, *said, "The reason that bouilla-baisse has a world reputation is because it is an aphrodisiac." Our seafood Bouillabaisse, my father François's version, features shellfish and julienned vegetables.*

THE BROTH:

$^1\!/_2$ cup olive oil

$^1\!/_2$ cup each finely chopped onion, carrots, and leeks, well-washed

$^1\!/_8$ cup finely julienned celery

2 teaspoons minced shallots

$^1\!/_2$ cup chopped fresh tomatoes

2 tablespoons tomato paste

$^1\!/_2$ cup dry white wine

1$^1\!/_2$ cups Fish Stock (page 235)

1 tablespoon sea salt (approximately)

1 *bouquet garni* consisting of $^1\!/_2$ teaspoon fennel seed, $^1\!/_2$ teaspoon anise seed, $^1\!/_2$ teaspoon cracked black peppercorns, 1 bay leaf, 1 clove, pinch of thyme, and 2 cloves garlic crushed, wrapped in a cheesecloth

$^1\!/_2$ teaspoon saffron

THE SEAFOOD:

6 mussels

4 little neck clams

$^1\!/_4$ pound sea scallops

1 1-pound Maine lobster

$^1\!/_4$ pound raw shrimp (20-24 count)

4 ounces fish fillets: red snapper, sea bass, grouper

4 oysters (optional)

2 teaspoons Pernod

2 teaspoons finely chopped fresh fennel

$^1\!/_2$ teaspoon chopped garlic

## TO PREPARE THE BROTH:

Heat the olive oil in a large saucepan or Dutch oven. Add the onions, leeks, celery, and carrots and cook covered until tender, about 15 minutes, stirring often. Add the shallots, tomatoes, tomato paste, white wine, fish stock, salt, and *bouquet garni*. Boil for approximately 25 minutes. Add the saffron and simmer 5 more minutes.

## TO PREPARE THE SEAFOOD:

While the broth is cooking, prepare the seafood.

Clean the mussels individually under cold running water, scraping off any clinging barnacles or "beards." Discard any half-open shells or any unusually heavy ones, indicating internal grit.

Rinse the clams, oysters, and scallops in cold water.

Using a sharp heavy knife, force the point of the blade through the top of the lobster head between the eyes; then cut down through the center of the head and tail, splitting the lobster in half. Remove and discard the lobster head and the intestinal vein running down the center of the tail. Remove the claws and crack them with the blunt edge of the blade.

Peel and devein the shrimp. Cut the fish fillets into 2-3-inch diagonal slices.

## TO PREPARE THE BOUILLABAISSE:

Add the mussels and clams to the boiling broth and simmer 5 minutes. Then add the lobster, shrimp, scallops, and fish. Continue boiling until all the shellfish are open, approximately 5-8 more minutes. Do not overcook.

Remove from heat, adjust seasoning (more garlic or saffron according to taste), add Pernod and chopped fennel, and serve immediately in large warm soup platters.

Garnish with garlic toasts.

*Hint:* Prepare the broth ahead and refrigerate. Reheat the broth and cook the seafood just prior to serving. Freeze any remaining broth to use another time.

# Rockfish with Vermouth Sauce

*Vermouth is not only used to make Martinis but also imparts a zesty accent to this sauce. Vermouth is an aromatized wine, flavored with herbs or spices.*

THE FISH:

>1  2-pound rockfish (8-10 ounces fillet)
>1 tablespoon butter
>1 tablespoon chopped shallots
>$^1/_3$ cup finely chopped onion
>$^1/_3$ cup finely diced carrot
>$^1/_3$ cup finely diced celery
>$^1/_3$ cup finely diced white of leek
>1 cup dry white wine
>$^1/_2$ teaspoon cracked peppercorns

THE SAUCE:

>$^1/_2$ cup heavy whipping cream
>1 tablespoon butter
>Pinch of cayenne pepper
>Sea salt
>Freshly ground pepper
>$1^1/_2$ tablespoons dry Vermouth
>2 teaspoons chopped chives

Filet the rockfish and skin the fillets. Cut each fillet into 3-4 slices. Cover and refrigerate.

With a cleaver or heavy knife, chop the head and bones of the rockfish. Place in a large bowl and rinse thoroughly under cold running water. Drain in a colander.

Place the butter in a saucepan just large enough to hold the fish bones. Just as the butter melts, add the minced shallots, $1/2$ of the prepared vegetables (carrot, celery, and leeks), and fish bones. Cook over high heat for 1 minute, stirring occasionally. Add the wine, and bring to a boil. Reduce heat to a slight boil, cover, and simmer for 10 minutes.

Strain the fish stock, place in a medium saucepan and reduce by two-thirds. Add the cream and bring to a boil. Remove from heat and whisk in the butter, a little at a time. Add the vermouth and cayenne pepper; taste and adjust seasonings.

Add the remaining diced vegetables and slices of fish to the sauce. Cook over low heat for approximately 3-4 minutes until the fish is just cooked through. Remove from heat.

Add the chopped chives. Taste and adjust seasonings.

*TO SERVE:*

Divide the fish and sauce between two warm shallow serving bowls.

*Hint:* If you prefer your fish without cream or butter, prepare the fish stock as above. Add double the amount of diced vegetables to the strained fish stock, the fish, and vermouth. Simmer until the fish is just cooked through. Taste and adjust seasonings. Serve as above.

# Monkfish with Bay Scallops and Champagne Sauce

*Scallops, Coquilles St. Jacques in French, were thus named because pilgrims to the shrine of St. Jacques (James) found these succulent mollusks in the nearby waters. We have two kinds available: the larger sea variety and the tiny sweet ones, from the bay. I favor the tiny succulent pearls from Nantucket.*

THE FISH:

> 1 pound monkfish
> $1/4$ pound bay scallops
> 2 tablespoons butter
> 2 teaspoons minced shallots
> 1 cup sliced raw white mushrooms (about $1/2$ pound)
> Sea salt
> Freshly ground pepper

THE SAUCE:

> $1/2$ cup champagne
> $1/2$ cup heavy whipping cream
> Sea salt
> Freshly ground pepper

## TO PREPARE THE FISH:

If not fileted, separate the 2 lobed fillets of the monkfish by removing the large spinal column. Cut away the dark outer skin and translucent gray inner skin, exposing the white flesh. Slice the fillets into $1/3$-inch thick medallions. Season with salt and pepper. Thoroughly wash the mushrooms, drain well, and season with salt and pepper.

Melt the 2 tablespoons of butter over low heat in a saucepan just large enough to hold the fish in 1 layer. Add the finely minced shallots, stirring them around the pan to coat the bottom evenly. Add the medallions of monkfish in 1 layer and cover with the seasoned sliced mushrooms. Pour the champagne over the fish, being careful not to disturb the mushrooms. Increase heat to high and bring wine to a boil.

Decrease heat to medium and boil gently for 1 minute. Add the seasoned bay scallops, cover, and simmer until just cooked through, about 2 minutes.

Remove fish and scallops with a slotted spatula and transfer to a serving platter. Cover and keep warm over a pan of simmering water.

### TO FINISH THE SAUCE:

Return saucepan over high heat and bring to boil. Reduce the liquid until it is almost dry, about 5 minutes. Add the cream and boil 1-2 minutes, until thick enough to coat a spoon. Remove the pan from the heat, taste, and adjust seasonings.

### TO SERVE:

Divide the fish, mushrooms, and scallops between two warm serving plates and set in the oven a few moments to heat, if necessary. Spoon the sauce over the fish and serve.

*Hint:* Monkfish becomes very tough if overcooked.

# Rare Salmon with Sherry Wine Vinegar

*Use wild salmon for the best color, flavor, and nutrition. Theoretically, a wild salmon is the best because it has been able to obtain its natural diet and survive in its normal environment.*

THE SALMON:

>2 4-5 ounce thick sliced salmon fillets
>10 white pearl onions
>4 small red bliss potatoes
>2 tablespoons butter
>Sea salt
>Freshly ground pepper
>1 tablespoon extra virgin olive oil

THE SAUCE:

>3 tablespoons sherry wine vinegar
>1 tablespoon soy sauce
>1/2 teaspoon finely minced shallots
>4 tablespoons butter
>2 teaspoons chopped chives
>Sea salt
>Freshly ground pepper
>1 small bunch bean or radish sprouts

Peel the potatoes, remove any "eyes" and cut each in half. Remove the outer layer from the pearl onions.

Place the onions and potatoes separately in small sauce pans just large enough to accommodate the vegetables; cover with cold water and add 1 tablespoon of butter and a pinch of sea salt to each. Place over high heat and bring to a boil. Boil uncovered to cook vegetables and evaporate the water. As liquid evaporates, reduce heat and allow vegetables to brown lightly. Onions require 10-12 minutes and potatoes approximately 15 minutes from the time the water boils. Be sure to watch carefully. Do not let the vegetables burn.

While the vegetables are cooking prepare the sauce.

## TO PREPARE THE SAUCE:

Place the sherry wine vinegar, soy sauce, and shallots in a small sauce pan and bring to a boil over high heat. Reduce by a third, remove from heat, and whisk in the 4 tablespoons butter. Taste and adjust seasonings. Add the prepared vegetables to the warm sauce, tossing to coat the vegetables.

## TO PREPARE THE SALMON:

*Preheat the broiler.*

Oil a small baking sheet, place the salmon fillets on the baking pan, and season with salt and pepper. Place under the broiler and cook for 3-4 minutes until partially cooked through.

## TO SERVE:

Place the cooked salmon fillets on two warm serving plates, divide the vegetables between the two plates, and sauce the plates. Sprinkle the chopped chives over the salmon and garnish the plates with a small bunch of fresh bean or radish sprouts. Serve at once.

*Variations:* Substitute or add other root vegetables such as carrots, turnips, rutabagas, parsnips, and kohlrabi, cooked in the same manner. Substitute red wine vinegar for the sherry wine vinegar.

# Dover Sole with Almonds and Asparagus Gratin

*Dover Sole, known properly as Sole de la Manche, is considered one of the finest fish in the world. Almonds are rich in protein and a valuable source of calcium, especially if eaten raw. Fresh asparagus are highly nutritious—rich in potassium, phosphorous, calcium, and rutin, a substance that helps maintain healthy blood vessels.*

THE GRATIN:

> 8-10 ounces large asparagus
> 1 teaspoon butter
> 1 medium egg
> ²/₃ cup heavy whipping cream
> Pinch of freshly ground nutmeg
> Sea salt
> Freshly ground pepper
> 2 tablespoons grated cheese (Parmesan or Gruyère)

THE SOLE:

> 2 14-16 ounce Dover soles, skinned and eviscerated
> ¹/₄ cup raw slivered almonds
> 4 tablespoons butter
> 1 tablespoon olive oil
> Sea salt
> Freshly ground pepper
> Flour
> 1 lemon

## TO PREPARE THE ASPARAGUS:

*Preheat oven to 425 degrees.*

Peel the asparagus, if desired, and cut off the tough lower stems. Steam the asparagus over salted water to blanch, about 2 minutes. Asparagus should remain fairly crisp. Drain at once on a towel.

Lightly butter a small ovenproof baking dish just large enough to accommodate the asparagus, about 9 x 6 x 1½ inches. Place the drained asparagus in the dish with the tips pointing in the same direction.

Place the egg in a small mixing bowl and whisk thoroughly. Add the cream, nutmeg, salt, and pepper, blending well. Taste and adjust seasonings. When salting the mixure, keep in mind that the cheese may be rather salty.

Just cover the asparagus with the seasoned mixture and sprinkle the cheese on top.

Bake in the preheated oven until the custard is set and nicely browned, about 15 minutes.

The gratin may be prepared ahead and reheated.

## TO PREPARE THE SOLE:

*Preheat the oven to 425 degrees.*

Salt, pepper, and dredge the soles in flour.

In a large sauté pan, heat 3 tablespoons of butter and 1 tablespoon of oil. As the butter begins to brown, place the prepared soles in the pan. Sauté the soles until the first side is brown, turn them over and place in the oven for approximately 5 minutes or until just cooked through. Remove from the oven and place on large sheet pan.

Using a pair of forks, separate the fillets and bones of each of the soles. Place each deboned sole on a large serving dish.

Melt the remaining butter in a medium skillet. When the butter has browned, add the slivered almonds and toss once or twice. Spoon the butter and almonds over the soles and serve warm with lemon wedges and the Asparagus Gratin.

*Variation:* If you prefer toasted almonds, spread the almonds in a single layer on a baking sheet and toast in the oven until lightly browned.

# Veal Scallopini with Gruyère Cheese

*A romantic Swiss custom was to put a wheel of cheese in storage the day a baby girl was born. This "wheel of romance" ripened in a cave until served at the daughter's wedding feast.*

> 1/2 pound veal scallopini (1 large or 2 small slices per person)
> Sea salt
> Freshly ground pepper
> Flour
> 2 tablespoons butter
> 1 teaspoon olive oil
> 3 tablespoons *Duxelles* (page 246)
> 2 slices ham (1 1/2 ounces each)
> 2 slices of Gruyère (1/8-inch thick, enough to cover the veal)
> 1/2 cup Basic Veal Sauce (page 232)
> 2 tablespoons sherry wine
> 1/2 cup heavy whipping cream

*Preheat the oven to 425 degrees*

Pound each slice of veal to a thickness of 1/8 - 1/4 inch using the flat side of a meat cleaver. Season both sides lightly with salt and pepper. Dredge in flour, shaking off the excess.

Heat the butter and oil in a large sauté pan over very high heat. When the butter begins to brown, sauté the prepared slices until lightly browned on both sides. Cooking time is less than a minute per side, as overcooking will toughen the meat.

Place the sautéed veal in the bottom of a buttered baking dish just large enough to hold the veal in a single layer.

Spread the *duxelles* over the prepared veal slices.

Place the ham over the veal and top with the cheese.

Heat the Veal Sauce to a boil and remove from heat. Add the heavy cream and season with salt, pepper, and sherry wine. Pour over the veal to just cover.

Place dish in preheated oven and bake until nicely browned, about 10 minutes. Remove from oven and transfer each portion to a warm plate. Serve.

# Lamb Chops with Barley

*Barley is one of civilization's oldest cultivated cereal grains. I prefer the fuller flavored hulled, rather than the nutritionally inferior pearled barley. Our ancestors believed that wearing a necklace made from rosemary kept one alert, young looking, and agile.*

THE LAMB:
>  1 rack of lamb
>  ¹/₂ teaspoon chopped fresh thyme
>  Sea salt
>  Freshly ground pepper
>  Olive oil

THE RED WINE REDUCTION:
>  Reserved lamb trimmings and bones
>  1 tablespoon finely minced onions
>  1 tablespoon finely diced carrot
>  1 teaspoon finely diced celery
>  1 cup hearty red wine
>  1 tablespoon butter (optional)
>  Sea salt
>  Freshly ground pepper
>  Pinch of thyme

THE BARLEY PILAF:
>  2 tablespoons butter
>  1 tablespoon finely chopped onion
>  ¹/₂ cup hulled barley
>  ³/₄ cup White Stock (page 228) or water
>  Sea salt
>  Freshly ground pepper

## TO PREPARE THE LAMB:

Trim the rack of lamb, removing excess fat and silver skin.

If bones are more than 3 inches long, cut shorter with a meat cleaver. Chop bones into ¹/₂-inch pieces. Reserve the lean trimmings and bones.

Cut into 6 chops and season with pepper and the chopped thyme.

Place chops in a shallow dish and coat with olive oil. Cover and refrigerate until ready to cook.

119

## TO PREPARE THE BARLEY:

*Preheat oven to 375 degrees.*

In a 1-quart saucepan melt, but do not brown, 1 tablespoon of the butter. Add the chopped onions and cook over low heat for 2-3 minutes until translucent. Stir occasionally.

Pour in the barley, thoroughly mixing with the butter and onions. Add the stock, chicken broth, or water to a level of ½-inch above the barley. Increase heat and bring to a boil. Season with salt and pepper, taste, and adjust. Tightly cover the pot and place in the oven for about 30 minutes, or until tender.

Remove the pan from the oven and spread the barley on a platter or small baking pan. Dice the remaining tablespoon of butter and gently fold into the hot barley with a fork. Correct seasonings. Return to pan and keep warm. The barley may be prepared ahead and reheated.

## TO COOK LAMB AND WINE REDUCTION:

Select a skillet or saucepan large enough to hold the lamb chops. Add 2 tablespoons olive oil to the skillet or saucepan.

Salt the lamb chops and sear in the hot pan. Sauté for about 2 minutes per side for medium-rare. Transfer the chops to a platter, cover, and keep warm in a very low oven.

Return the pan to high heat and immediately add the reserved scraps and bones to the skillet, maintaining at high heat. Brown well, stirring occasionally, for about 3-4 minutes. Add the chopped vegetables and sauté another minute.

Tilt pan and carefully pour out as much grease as possible.

Return the drained bones and trimmings to the pan.

Deglaze the pan with the red wine. Reduce by two-thirds and strain into a bowl. Stir in the butter, if desired, and adjust seasonings.

## TO SERVE:

Divide the warm barley between two warm plates.

Arrange the lamb chops on the serving plates. Pour sauce around the chops.

Garnish the plates with fresh sprigs of thyme, rosemary, or mint.

# Grilled Rib-Eye
# of American Kobe Beef
# with Niçoise Vegetables

*Kobe beef is an exclusive grade of beef. Originally raised in Kobe, Japan, it is now also produced in the United States. These pampered cattle are massaged with sake and fed a special diet that includes beer. This specialized treatment results in extraordinarily tender and full-flavored beef. Niçoise is the name given to various dishes typical of the Provence region around Nice, in which the most common ingredients are garlic, olives, basil, tomatoes, peppers, and often anchovies. The fennel adds a licorice-like flavor to this dish.*

THE NIÇOISE VEGETABLES:

     1 medium fennel bulb ($^1/_3$ cup)
     1 small red bell pepper( $^1/_3$ cup)
     1 small yellow bell pepper ($^1/_3$ cup)
     1 small green bell pepper ($^1/_3$ cup)
     1 medium onion ($^1/_3$ cup)
     1 medium tomato ($^1/_3$ cup)
     2 tablespoons extra virgin olive oil
     1 teaspoon finely minced basil
     $^1/_2$ teaspoon minced garlic
     2 tablespoons sliced Calamata olives
     Sea salt
     Freshly ground pepper

THE HORSERADISH SAUCE:

     $^1/_3$ cup whipped cream
     1 tablespoon grated horseradish
     $^1/_4$ teaspoon red wine vinegar
     Sea salt
     Freshly ground pepper
     Pinch of cayenne pepper

THE BEEF:

> 1 trimmed 16-18 ounce boneless rib-eye steak (Kobe beef)
> Sea salt
> Freshly ground pepper
> Olive oil

## TO PREPARE THE VEGETABLES:

Thinly slice the onion and fennel bulb. Split, seed, and thinly slice the peppers and tomato. Place a large saucepan over high heat and add the olive oil. Add the onion, peppers, fennel, and tomato. Cover and cook 4-5 minutes, until the vegetables are *al dente*. Remove from heat and add the basil, garlic, and olives. Season with salt and pepper.

## TO PREPARE THE SAUCE:

Combine all ingredients. Mix gently but thoroughly.

Taste and adjust seasonings.

## TO PREPARE THE BEEF:

*Preheat the grill*

Season with salt and pepper and lightly coat with olive oil.

Grill approximately 7 minutes per side for medium rare.

Let steak rest for at least 5 minutes before slicing.

## TO ASSEMBLE:

Make a nest of vegetables on two warm plates and then top with slices of beef. Drizzle sauce around the beef and vegetables.

*Hint:* The Niçoise vegetables may be prepared ahead and reheated. They may also be seasoned with homemade Vinaigrette (page 245) and served cold.

# Roast Pork Tenderloin with Alsatian Potato Pancake

*A thoughtful Roman host served cabbage, believing it prevented hangovers. This recipe is a classic example of how Alsatian chefs have harmoniously blended the culinary traditions of France and Germany.*

THE PORK:

> 1 pork tenderloin (12 ounces)
> Sea salt
> Freshly ground pepper
> 2 tablespoons olive oil
> $\frac{1}{2}$ cup Pork Sauce (page 239)

THE PANCAKE:

> 1 medium Russet potato, 8 ounces
> 1 medium egg
> 2 tablespoons flour
> Sea salt
> Freshly ground pepper
> $\frac{1}{3}$ cup sauerkraut
> 1 tablespoon butter
> 1 teaspoon olive oil

## TO PREPARE THE PORK:

*Preheat oven to 425 degrees.*

Trim excess fat and silver skin from the tenderloin. Season the pork with salt and pepper.

Place a skillet large enough to hold the tenderloin over high heat and add the olive oil. When the oil just begins to smoke, add the tenderloin.

Sear for 2 minutes per side, browning nicely. Place the skillet in the preheated oven for about 10 minutes, until the pork is just cooked through. Internal temperature should reach 160 degrees. While the pork is roasting, prepare the pancake.

## TO PREPARE THE PANCAKE:

*Preheat oven to 400 degrees.*

Peel, wash, and grate the potato. Place the grated potato in a strainer and add ¹/₂ teaspoon of salt; mix thoroughly and allow to drain for a few minutes. Press the grated potato to remove excess moisture.

Beat the egg in a small mixing bowl with a wire whisk. Mix in the flour, add the grated potato, and season with pepper and more salt, if desired.

Heat the butter and oil in a well seasoned or non-stick 6-8 inch sauté pan. When the butter begins to brown, place ¹/₂ of the potato mix in the pan and press to form a pancake. Cover the potato with the sauerkraut and cover the layer of the sauerkraut with the remaining potato mix.

Sauté each side until golden brown, about 2 minutes per side, and place pan in the preheated oven for about 6 minutes or until the potato is cooked through. Keep warm.

Cut pancake in half just before serving.

## TO SERVE:

Heat the sauce.

Remove pork from oven and allow to rest at least 5 minutes before slicing.

Slice and arrange on two warm plates. Then place half of the pancake on each plate and pour warm sauce over the sliced meat.

# Coffee-Marinated Veal Chops with Parsnip Gratin

*Parsnips were one of the most popular vegetables in Europe until it was eclipsed by the potato, brought from the new world. The sweet nutlike flavor of parsnips is a taste treat too few people are familiar with today. The coffee imparts an enticing flavor and appealing color to the veal.*

### THE VEAL:

> 2 cups freshly brewed coffee (strong), cooled
> 2 veal chops, trimmed
> 2 tablespoons oil
> 1 tablespoon butter
> Sea salt
> Freshly ground pepper

### THE PARSNIP GRATIN:

> ½ pound parsnips
> ½ cup heavy whipping cream
> 3 tablespoons grated cheese (Parmesan or Gruyère)
> ¼ teaspoon finely minced garlic
> Sea salt
> Freshly ground pepper

## TO MARINATE THE VEAL:

Place the veal chops in a loaf pan or dish just large enough to hold them. Cover with the coffee. Marinate for 2 days, turning the chops every day.

## TO PREPARE THE GRATIN:

*Preheat oven to 425 degrees.*

Peel parsnips and thinly slice into rounds. Place the sliced parsnips in a mixing bowl and add the garlic, salt, and pepper. Toss ingredients to mix thoroughly.

Butter the bottom and sides of a small baking dish. Place parsnips in the dish and pour the heavy cream over the parsnips and cover with the cheese.

Place the dish in the preheated oven for 30 minutes or until well browned.

May be prepared ahead and reheated.

## TO PREPARE THE VEAL CHOPS:

*Preheat oven to 425 degrees.*

Remove the chops from the coffee and pat dry.

Place the butter and oil in a sauté pan large enough to accommodate the 2 veal chops. Place the pan over high heat, when the butter begins to brown, add the chops. Brown thoroughly on one side 2-3 minutes and turn the chops over. Place the pan in preheated oven for approximately 10-12 minutes until the chops are just cooked through.

Serve with Parsnip Gratin.

*Hint:* Decaffeinated coffee will work just as well.

# Pepper Steaks with Fennel and Garlic Purée

*Pepper has long since been considered a favorite spice throughout the world. Widely used in the East, it is believed that Alexander the Great introduced it to Europe. In Medieval time, Europeans believed pepper to ignite passion. Similarly, in the middle ages, garlic was thought to enhance romantic feelings, as suggested in Boccaccio's Decameron, in which a man sends his beloved a gift of garlic and wins her love.*

THE PURÉE:

    1 large fennel bulb (6 ounces)
    3 ounces peeled potatoes ($^1/_3$ cup)
    $^1/_2$ cup water
    $^1/_2$ teaspoon lemon juice
    1 rounded tablespoon chopped onion
    1 ounce whole peeled garlic cloves (7)
    Sea salt
    Freshly ground pepper
    1 tablespoon butter
    1 tablespoon heavy whipping cream

THE STEAKS:

    2 New York strip steaks (8-10 ounces each)
    Sea salt
    1 tablespoon cracked black peppercorns
    1 tablespoon butter
    2 tablespoons oil

THE SAUCE:

    1 heaping tablespoon green peppercorns (drain brine)
    1 shot cognac
    $^1/_2$ teaspoon Dijon-style mustard
    $^1/_2$ cup heavy whipping cream
    2 tablespoons Basic Beef Sauce (page 232)
    Sea salt
    Freshly ground pepper

## TO PREPARE THE PURÉE:

Trim the stem and any blemished outer layer of the fennel bulb to obtain 1 cup of cleaned fennel. Reserve and chop 1 tablespoon of any of the fine green stems that may be attached to the bulbs. Thinly slice the cleaned fennel and potatoes and place in a medium saucepan. Add the water, lemon juice, and pinch of salt and pepper.

Place over high heat and bring to a boil. Reduce heat and cover. Boil gently for about 25 minutes until the fennel is very tender and most of the water absorbed.

While the fennel is steaming, place the garlic cloves on a small sheet pan and bake in a preheated 350 degree oven for approximately 30 minutes until tender and lightly browned. Reduce heat and cover if garlic browns too quickly.

Place the fennel, without draining, in a food processor with the roasted garlic. Purée for about 1 minute or until blended completely. Stop processor and add the butter and heavy cream and process for 10 seconds. Taste and adjust seasonings. Sprinkle chopped fennel on the purée before serving.

## TO PREPARE THE STEAK AND SAUCE:

Lightly salt the steaks. Using the heel of your hand, firmly press the cracked peppercorns into both sides of each steak.

Heat the butter and oil in a heavy skillet. When the butter begins to brown, add the steaks and cook over high heat until they are browned on both sides. Allow approximately 2 minutes per side for medium rare.

Remove steaks from skillet and pour off the grease. Return steaks to skillet, place over high heat, and flambè with green peppercorn and cognac mixture. Again, remove steaks from the pan and keep warm while you prepare the sauce.

Return skillet to high heat, add cream, mustard, and Beef Sauce. Boil several minutes, reducing volume by about half. Taste and adjust seasonings. Pour sauce around steaks and serve with the fennel and garlic purée.

*Variation:* Substitute cracked black peppercorns for the green peppercorns in the sauce.

# Beer Ice Cream

*Beer is no doubt the most widespread and the oldest alcoholic drink in the world. The first traces of "liquid bread" based on fermented cereals were found in Mesopotamia and Egypt. I tasted this uniquely-flavored ice cream in Alsace.*

Makes 1½ quarts:

> 2 cups milk
> 6 medium egg yolks
> 1 cup evaporated cane juice or sugar
> 2 cups heavy whipping cream
> 2 cups dark beer

Scald the milk in a heavy stainless steel pan.

Beat the egg yolks and sugar together in a glass or stainless bowl until the mixture whitens.

Slowly pour the hot milk into the egg yolk mixture, whisking constantly. Transfer the mixture back to the saucepan. Cook over simmering water or very low direct heat until the custard thickens and coats a spoon, but do not boil. Immediately pour in the heavy cream. Add the beer.

Strain the custard into a bowl, cool, and refrigerate.

Freeze the custard according to the directions for your machine.

Place in a covered freezer container and harden before serving.

# Warm Chocolate Tart

*The combination of chocolate and love is a double whammy. Chocolate contains caffeine-like substances which excite the system as well as the taste buds. There is nothing like a warm tart for dessert.*

> 1 6-7 inch Sweet Pie Crust (page 247)
> ½ cup heavy whipping cream
> ⅓ cup milk
> 8 ounces semi-sweet chocolate
> 2 whole eggs

*Preheat oven to 350 degrees.*

Combine the heavy cream and milk in a heavy saucepan.

Place over high heat and bring contents to a boil. Remove from heat, add the chocolate, and stir until the chocolate is completely melted.

Beat the 2 eggs in a bowl. Slowly pour the warm chocolate and cream mixture into the bowl, whisking constantly.

Pour the contents into the Sweet Pie Crust and bake in preheated oven for approximately 10 minutes until the custard is set. Test for doneness by inserting a toothpick into the custard. The custard is ready if toothpick comes out clean. Remove from oven and serve warm with ice cream, if desired.

*Variation:* Garnish with a few fresh raspberries, a great combination.

# Quince Crème Brûlée

*The literal translation of crème brûlée, a rich velvety dessert, is "burnt cream." The custard is chilled and sprinkled with sugar just before serving. The sugar topping is quickly caramelized with a torch or under a boiler. This yields a warm brittle layer of caramel blanketing a creamy custard. The slight tartness of the quince balances the sweet custard.*

## THE QUINCE:

> 1 quince
> 1/2 cup water
> 1/3 cup evaporated cane juice or sugar
> 1 clove
> Pinch of cinnamon

## THE CUSTARD:

> 2 large eggs
> 2 tablespoons evaporated cane juice or sugar
> 1/2 cup heavy whipping cream
> 1/2 cup beer
> 1/2 teaspoon vanilla extract
> Pinch cinnamon

## TO PREPARE THE QUINCE:

Combine the water, evaporated cane juice, clove, and cinnamon and bring to a boil over high heat. Reduce flame and simmer for 3-4 minutes. Peel quince, quarter, and core. Cut each quarter into 4 thin slices and add them to the syrup. Simmer gently until the quince slices are tender but slightly firm, approximately 4 minutes depending on the ripeness of the fruit. Remove quince slices from the syrup; cool and drain. May be prepared ahead of time.

Cover and refrigerate.

## TO PREPARE THE CUSTARD:

*Preheat the oven to 275 degrees*

Beat the eggs in a medium glass or stainless steel bowl and thoroughly whisk in the evaporated cane juice. Add the remaining ingredients, mixing completely.

Divide the thoroughly drained quince sections into two shallow oven-proof ramekins (1 cup size by volume). Place the quince in a single layer in the bottom of the ramekins.

Set the prepared ramekins into a baking dish or pan, at least 1-inch deep. Fill the ramekins with the custard mix. Pour hot water into the baking dish to a level halfway up the sides of the ramekins.

Carefully, place the baking dish in the preheated oven and bake for about 35 minutes, until the custards are set. Test for doneness by inserting a small knife into one of the custards. The custards are set if the blade comes out clean.

Remove from the oven and lift the ramekins out of the water bath and cool.

Scatter 2 tablespoons evaporated cane juice or sugar over each and place under a preheated broiler to melt and lightly brown the sugar.

*Hint:* The evaporated cane juice does not caramelize quite as well as white sugar.

# Snow Eggs

*Named Oeufs À La Neige or Île Flottante in French, snow eggs are a very light dessert made from stiffly beaten egg whites and sweetener. The poached meringues are drizzled with caramel and placed in a pool of custard sauce. This classic recipe is an especially appropriate ending to a romantic repast.*

THE POACHING SYRUP:

> 1 quart water
> 1/2 cup evaporated cane juice or sugar

THE MERINGUE:

> Pinch of sea salt
> 3 large egg whites
> 5 tablespoons evaporated cane juice or sugar
> 1/2 teaspoon grated lemon rind
> 1/2 teaspoon grated orange rind
> 1/2 teaspoon vanilla extract

THE GLAZE:

> 1/3 cup evaporated cane juice or sugar
> 3 tablespoons water

THE SAUCE:

> 1/2 cup Vanilla Custard Sauce (page 252)
> 1/2 tablespoon *Kirsch* (cherry brandy)

## TO PREPARE THE POACHING MEDIUM:

Combine water and sweetener in a shallow saucepan, approximately 10-inch diameter x 3-inches deep. Bring to a boil over high heat. Reduce to very low heat and allow to simmer while preparing the egg whites for the meringue.

## TO PREPARE THE MERINGUE:

Combine the egg whites and salt in the bowl of an electric mixer. Whip on high speed until just foamy white. Continue whipping while slowly adding the evaporated cane juice, 1 tablespoon at a time. Beat until the meringue mixture forms stiff glossy peaks.

Reduce speed and add the remaining ingredients whipping 3-4 turns to blend thoroughly.

## TO COOK THE "DUMPLINGS":

Maintain heat under saucepan so syrup just simmers. Dip a large kitchen spoon into the simmering syrup.

Scoop out a "dumpling" of meringue by placing the spoon in the meringue mixture with the edge of the spoon horizontal to the side of the bowl. Form the dumpling by bringing up the spoon against the side of the bowl, thereby "curling" the meringue into the desired shape.

Carefully place spoon into simmering liquid to slide dumpling off. Repeat above forming 4 dumplings. Allow snow eggs to cook about 2 minutes before turning over by flipping with the spoon. Simmer another 2 minutes and carefully spoon the snow eggs out of the liquid onto a cloth to drain.

Place drained snow eggs on serving platter and prepare the caramel.

## TO PREPARE THE CARAMEL GLAZE:

Combine the water and evaporated cane juice in a small heavy saucepan. Place over high heat and boil, shaking the pan occasionally, until the granules melt and caramelize to a golden brown. Watch carefully, as the difference between golden brown and burned glaze is a matter of seconds. The caramel will continue to cook in the pan after it has been removed from the heat. Dip the bottom half of the pan in a large bowl of cold water to cool slightly. Immediately, pour over the snow eggs.

All the glaze may not be required.

## TO SERVE:

Pour the *Kirsch*-flavored sauce around the snow eggs and serve.

*Variation:* You may melt a rich vanilla ice cream rather than make the vanilla custard sauce.

# Individual Warm Apple Tarts

*The apple has embodied desire throughout history. In the allegorical story associated with the Garden of Eden, Eve tempted Adam with an apple and a piece of it became lodged in his throat, forming a reminder for all-time, the Adam's apple.*

*Preheat oven to 450 degrees.*

> 2 Granny Smith or Golden Delicious apples, peeled, cored and
>    cut into 6 sections
> 2 tablespoons unsalted butter
> 2 tablespoons evaporated cane juice or sugar
> Pinch of cinnamon
> 2 5-inch diameter by $1/8$-inch disks of Sweet Pie Crust (page 247)
> Crème fraîche

Brown the butter in a heavy medium sauté pan over high heat.

Add the apple wedges and sprinkle with the evaporated cane juice. Cook over high heat, allowing the evaporated cane juice to caramelize. Toss the apples several times. When the evaporated cane juice is caramelized, add the cinnamon, toss, and remove apples from pan.

Allow the apples to cool enough to handle; slice each apple section into 4 thin slices. Arrange the apple slices on the disks of dough. Bake in the hot oven for about 12 minutes until the dough is nicely browned on the bottom.

Remove from the oven and serve while still warm.

Garnish with crème fraîche or rich vanilla ice cream.

# Celebrations

For life's special moments you pull out all the stops.

Perhaps you are commemorating the most important anniversary for lovers, the day you first gazed upon each other. Maybe you are lucky enough to have been together for many, many years and have a lifetime of memories.

These are meals for your most romantic of days, the moments that mean so much to you both. These festive occasions demand some extra preparation time and expense, but will never fail to demonstrate your deep affection.

Celebrating a birthday? She assumed that you were going out to dinner, but will be delighted that you are doing the cooking.

I recommend you bring your sweetheart right into the kitchen. Because you have done the prep work earlier, only the finishing touches need to be completed in front of admiring eyes.

I'm certain that preparing this meal for your special someone will convince him or her of the depth of your love.

# Suggested Menus

◆◆◆

Truffles in Puff Pastry
Lobster with Sauternes Sauce
Baked Alaska

Wild Mushroom Napoleon
Fillets of Sole with Oysters
Molten Chocolate Cake

Cream of Pike Soup
Medallions of Texas Antelope
Truffle Ice Cream

Duck Flan with Sweet and Sour Sauce
Beef Baked in a Salt Crust
Champagne Mousse

Terrine of Foie Gras
Poached Beef Tenderloin
Crêpes Suzettes

# Cream of Pike Soup
# with Olive Quenelles

*My version of a soup by Antoine Westerman from his Michelin three-star restaurant in Strasbourg, France. Pike is a freshwater fish with a long head and strong jaws equipped with hundreds of small sharp teeth.*

THE SOUP:

    1 1/2 tablespoons butter
    1/3 cup *mirepoix*, consisting of a combination of finely diced
        celery, carrots, onion, and leeks
    1 tablespoon flour
    1/2 cup dry Alsatian white wine (Pinot Blanc)
    2 cups fresh Fish Stock made with pike bones (page 235)
    1/2 teaspoon cracked peppercorns
    1 sprig of fresh tarragon
    1/3 cup heavy whipping cream

THE OLIVE QUENELLES:

    1/2 cup Calamata olives

## TO PREPARE THE SOUP:

In a heavy saucepan melt the butter, add the *mirepoix*, and sweat on low heat for approximately 6 minutes, until tender. Add the flour, mix thoroughly, and cook for 30 seconds, being careful not to scorch flour. Add the white wine, whisk completely, and bring to a boil. Add the fish stock and bring to a boil, reduce flame, and simmer for 30 minutes, whisking occasionally.

Strain soup through a fine strainer. Add the heavy whipping cream.

Taste and adjust seasonings.

## TO PREPARE THE OLIVE QUENELLES:

Pit and finely chop the olives.

Place minced olives in a small heavy saucepan and heat over medium flame for 1-2 minutes to release the oils. The chopped olives should resemble coffee grounds. While warm and using a demitasse spoon, shape the minced olives into dumplings. Store on wax paper and cover until ready to use.

## TO SERVE:

Ladle soup into warm bowls and float quenelles in warm soup just before serving.

# Truffled Duck Consommé

*A warning about truffles: the musky sensual essence reputedly inflames the senses. They are the "black diamonds" of cookery.*

Makes 2 quarts:

> 3-4 pounds duck (chicken) bones and wings
> 3 quarts cold water (approximately)
> ½ cup dry white wine
> 2 medium onions
> 4 cloves
> 1 celery stalk
> 1 white section of one leek
> 1 large carrot
> 1 small bunch of parsley stems
> 2 bay leaves
> Pinch of thyme
> 1 tablespoon sea salt
> 1 teaspoon cracked peppercorns
> 1 ounce of peeled black truffle

*STEP 1:*

Cut 1 onion in half and press 2 cloves into the top of each. Place each half, cut side down, over direct high heat and char, approximately 4-5 minutes or until the onion is burned and very dark.

Crack the bones with the aid of a cleaver. Cut the vegetables into large pieces.

Place bones and vegetables in a large stock pot, cover with cold water and bring to a boil over high heat. Skim away fat and scum with a ladle.

Lower heat and simmer uncovered for ½ hour, skimming as needed.

Add the remaining ingredients and simmer another 3 hours, skimming as needed. Add water during simmering, if necessary. Approximately 2 quarts should remain.

Strain the broth, taste, and adjust seasonings.

> ¹/₂ pound lean ground duck (chicken)
> 6 egg whites
> 2 tablespoons chopped celery
> 2 tablespoons chopped carrot
> 2 tablespoons chopped onion
> 1 clove
> 1 bay leaf
> Sprig of thyme

Mix all of the other ingredients together in the bottom of a large pot. Add the duck broth and place over high heat. When the broth begins to boil, reduce heat and simmer for about 2 hours to clarify and strengthen the consommé. Do not stir the broth while simmering, so as not to disturb the meat and egg mass.

Taste consommé and adjust seasonings.

Place a large piece of damp gauze or cloth over a strainer resting over a pot or bowl and slowly pour the consommé through the gauze. Try not to disturb the ground meat and egg mass.

Refrigerate the strained consommé. Scrape any fat from the surface of the congealed consommé before using.

Cut the truffles into a thick dice. Divide and place in the bottom of the serving bowls.

Ladle the hot seasoned consommé into the warm prepared bowls and serve at once.

*Hint:* If using cooked truffles, add some of the cooking liquid to flavor the consommé.

*Variation:* Other garnishes such as julienne duck meat or black trumpet mushrooms may be used to garnish the soup.

# Truffles in Puff Pastry

*This recipe was the specialty of the house when I worked in Paris at the Rôtisserie Périgourdine. The restaurant is now a bistro but the memory of the savory and mysterious truffle aroma remains.*

>    3 ounces chicken breast or veal
>    1 ounce fresh duck *foie gras*
>    1 medium egg
>    ½ tablespoon heavy whipping cream
>    Sea salt
>    Freshly ground pepper
>    Pinch of Pâté Spices (page 228) or nutmeg
>    2 1-ounce fresh truffles
>    8 ounces Puff Pastry (page 248)
>    1 egg, beaten

Wash, brush, and peel the truffles. Finely chop the truffle peelings and set aside.

To prepare the stuffing, place the chicken breast and *foie gras* in the bowl of a small food processor fitted with the steel blade.

Process for about 30 seconds until smooth and add the egg, truffle peelings, cream, salt, pepper, and pinch of Pâté Spices and process a few seconds to mix well. Sauté a small amount of the mixture, taste, and adjust seasonings. Refrigerate.

*Preheat oven to 375 degrees.*

To prepare the truffles, roll out the puff pastry into a sheet approximately 10-inches by 10-inches by ½-inch. Using a 5-inch round dough cutter, cut 4 disks of puff pastry.

Beat the egg in a small bowl with a fork. Brush 2 sections of dough with the beaten egg.

Divide the prepared stuffing in two and completely envelope the truffles in the stuffing. Set each prepared truffle in the center of a section of prepared dough. Cover each truffle with a disk of the remaining dough. Firmly press the edges of dough together. Brush the puff pastry with the remaining beaten egg.

Bake the puff pastry-enrobed truffles in the preheated oven for about 20 minutes until the pastry is nicely browned. If the pastry browns much sooner, the oven is too hot. Cover with foil and reduce heat. Serve immediately.

Serve with Truffle Sauce (page 234)

# Wild Mushroom Napoleon

*Throughout history, mushrooms have been regarded as food of the gods. This is a non-traditional Napoleon, as we will use potato crisps (don't call them chips) instead of the usual puff pastry. A shimmering port wine reduction moistens the Napoleon, enhancing the mushrooms' flavors.*

THE NAPOLEON:

> 1 large Russet potato
> Olive oil
> Sea salt

THE FILLING:

> 4-6 jumbo asparagus
> 1/2 pound assorted mushrooms: Morel, Shiitake, Oyster
> 2 tablespoons olive oil
> 1 rounded teaspoon finely chopped shallots
> Pinch of finely minced garlic
> Sea salt
> Freshly ground pepper

THE SAUCE:

> 1/2 cup port wine
> 1 teaspoon balsamic vinegar
> 1 teaspoon butter
> Sea salt
> Freshly ground pepper

## TO PREPARE THE POTATO CRISPS:

*Preheat the oven to 375 degrees.*

Wash and peel the potato. Using a very sharp knife or vegetable slicer, cut 8 paper-thin lengthwise slices of potato.

Lightly coat the bottom of cookie sheet with the olive oil.

Place the slices of potato on the prepared baking sheet.

Brush the slices of potato with olive oil.

Bake in the preheated oven for approximately 10 minutes until the slices are lightly browned and crisp.

Carefully transfer the baked potato slices, using a wide spatula, onto paper towels to remove excess oil. Season with salt and set aside.

## TO PREPARE THE VEGETABLE FILLING:

Trim the stems and steam the asparagus over salted water for 3-4 minutes, *al dente*. Drain and reserve. Trim, wash, and drain the assorted mushrooms. Heat the olive oil in a medium sauté pan, add the prepared mushrooms, and sauté for 2-3 minutes over high flame, tossing occasionally. Add the shallots and cook 1 more minute. Add a pinch of garlic and season with salt and pepper. Toss several times and remove from heat. Transfer the sautéed mushrooms to a plate and keep warm.

## TO PREPARE THE SAUCE:

Place the same sauté pan in which you cooked the mushrooms over high heat. Add the port wine and vinegar. Bring to a boil and reduce by half to obtain about $1/4$ cup port wine reduction, approximately 4 minutes.

Remove from heat and whisk in the butter.

Taste and adjust seasonings. Keep warm.

## TO ASSEMBLE THE NAPOLEON:

Place a potato crisp in the center of each of two warm plates.

Place $1/2$ of the prepared asparagus over each of the 2 potato crisps.

Divide $1/2$ of the sautéed mushrooms to cover each of the potato crisps.

Place another potato crisp over the mushrooms and repeat the previous step. Finally, top the second layer of mushrooms with the third slice of potato. (The 2 extra slices of potato are insurance against breakage.)

Spoon $1/2$ of the port wine sauce around each of the Napoleons and serve.

*Hint:* Wild mushrooms—Morels, Chanterelles, Cèpes, Hedgehog, Chicken of the Woods, Lobster, and Cauliflower—are plentiful seasonally throughout the year. Mix several varieties with the addition of domestic mushrooms for a memorable dish. Sauté the mushrooms over very high heat. If necessary, prepare in several batches, as the mushrooms will boil rather than sauté if overcrowded in the pan.

# Pike Quenelles

*Traditionally, Quenelles are dumplings made with finely ground meat or fish bound with fat and eggs. They are then molded into small sausage or egg shapes and poached. The name comes from the German word* Knodell *for dumpling.*

> 4 ounces firm white fish fillet: rockfish, seabass, or grouper
> 1 medium egg
> $\frac{1}{3}$ cup heavy whipping cream
> $\frac{1}{2}$ teaspoon cognac
> Sea salt
> Freshly ground pepper
> Pinch of cayenne pepper
> 4 ounces Lobster Sauce (page 236)

### TO PREPARE THE FISH MOUSSE:

Remove any bones or skin that might remain on the fish.

Cut the fish into 1-inch pieces and place in the bowl of a food processor. Purée the fish in the food processor fitted with a steel blade. With the processor running, add the egg and process until the egg is completely blended into the fish. Slowly pour in the heavy cream (with machine running) until completely incorporated. Add the remaining ingredients and give the mousse a final spin to blend. Poach a small amount of the mousse in lightly salted water and taste. Adjust seasonings, if necessary. Chill completely.

### TO PREPARE THE QUENELLES:

Bring 1 quart of lightly salted water to a boil. Reduce heat to a simmer.

Maintain heat under saucepan so the water just simmers. Dip a large kitchen or serving spoon into the simmering water.

Scoop out a "dumpling" of mousse by placing the spoon in the mousse mixture with the edge of the spoon horizontal to the side of the bowl. Form the dumpling by bringing up the spoon against the side of the bowl thereby "curling" the mousse into the desired shape.

Carefully place the spoon into simmering liquid to slide dumpling off. Repeat above, forming 4 dumplings. Allow the quenelles to cook about 2 minutes before turning over by flipping with the spoon. Simmer another 2 minutes and carefully spoon the quenelles out of the liquid onto a cloth to drain.

## TO SERVE:

*Preheat the oven to 450 degrees.*

Divide the lobster sauce between two small ovenproof dishes.

Place 2 of the quenelles in each dish. Bake in the oven for about 7 minutes until the quenelles rise and begin to brown slightly. Serve immediately.

# Duck Flan with Sweet and Sour Sauce and Shallot Confit

*These velvety flans have a smooth texture and irresistible aroma. Confit is actually an ancient method of preserving surplus foods at harvest time. The unique flavor of confit is the rasion d'être in modern times.*

THE FLAN:

    4 duck livers or 5-6 chicken livers (3 ounces)
    Sea salt
    Freshly ground pepper
    1 tablespoon armagnac or cognac
    1 tablespoon butter
    1 teaspoon oil
    1/2 teaspoon finely minced shallots
    Pinch of chopped garlic
    Pinch of nutmeg
    Pinch of cayenne
    1 whole large egg
    1/2 cup heavy whipping cream

THE SWEET AND SOUR DUCK SAUCE:

    2 tablespoons evaporated cane juice or sugar
    1/2 cup red wine vinegar
    1/2 cup diced apple (approximately 1/2 medium apple)
    1/2 cup Duck Stock (page 231)
    1/2 teaspoon Calvados or apple brandy
    1 teaspoon crème fraîche
    Sea salt
    Freshly ground pepper

THE SHALLOT CONFIT:

    2 ounces shallots (4 medium shallots)
    1/2 cup rendered goose or duck fat, lard, or olive oil
        (enough to cover shallots completely)

*TO PREPARE THE FLANS:*

Rinse the livers and drain well. Remove any sinews or green bile.

Place the cleaned livers in a small bowl, add the armagnac, and marinate at least 3 hours or overnight.

*Preheat the oven to 350 degrees.*

Drain the livers, reserving the marinade. Season with salt and pepper.

Heat 1 tablespoon of butter and 1 teaspoon of oil in a small sauté pan over high heat. When the butter begins to brown, add the seasoned livers, and brown on both sides, about 30 seconds per side. Add the shallots and toss in the pan several times. Livers should remain rare.

Immediately transfer the sautéed livers into the bowl of a food processor fitted with the steel blade. Be sure to scrape all the shallots and liquids from the sauté pan onto the livers. Add the pinch of nutmeg, garlic, cayenne, salt, and pepper and process for 1 minute until smooth.

Transfer the contents of the food processor to a mixing bowl.

Thoroughly whisk the eggs and add to the processed livers along with the cream and reserved marinade. Whisk completely. Taste for seasoning by cooking about 1 teaspoon of the liver purée in a lightly buttered sauté pan over low heat until set. Adjust seasonings.

Butter two ½-cup size porcelain molds or ramekins. Fill with the prepared mixture and place in a shallow pan.

Pour hot tap water into the shallow pan containing the molds to a level halfway up the sides of the molds. Place over high heat and bring the water in the pan to a boil. Immediately transfer the pan to preheated oven and bake for approximately 25 minutes until the flans are set and feel firm to the touch. Test by inserting a tooth pick which should come out clean.

Remove the pan from the oven, leave the ramekins in the pan, and allow to cool for another 5 minutes.

## TO PREPARE THE SAUCE:

Heat the evaporated cane juice to a light caramel in a small heavy saucepan over medium heat. Immediately add the diced apple and vinegar. Boil until the caramel is dissolved. Add the Duck Stock and boil uncovered for 3-4 minutes, reducing the volume by one-quarter. Remove from heat, add the Calvados and crème fraîche. Taste and adjust seasonings.

*Variation:* Use chicken in place of the duck stock.

## TO PREPARE THE SHALLOTS:

Peel the shallots. In a small heavy saucepan over low flame, heat the fat to about 100 degrees, just warm to the touch. Add the shallots and toss thoroughly to completely cover the shallots with the fat. Bring to a light boil, simmer until soft and translucent, approximately $1/2$ hour. Remove from heat, allowing the shallots to remain in the fat. Reheat in the fat and drain well before serving.

## TO SERVE:

Reheat flans, if prepared ahead, by simmering in a *bain-marie* for about 5 minutes.

Place a warm serving plate upside down over a ramekin and invert. Lift off the mold and pour the sauce around the flan. Garnish with shallot *confit* and serve at once.

# Terrine of Foie Gras

*The fattening of the goose or duck to enlarge the liver was recorded as early as Egyptian times. This terrine is one of the most delicious and sensuous creations on the planet. A gift par excellence for that special someone.*

> 1 fresh A grade duck *foie gras* (about 1-1¹/₂ pounds)
> The following are per pound of *foie gras*:
> 1¹/₂ teaspoons sea salt
> ¹/₈ teaspoon freshly ground pepper
> 1¹/₂ teaspoons evaporated cane juice or brown sugar
> Pinch of nutmeg or Pâté Spices (page 228)
> 1¹/₂ teaspoons Cognac

## TO PREPARE THE LIVER:

Weigh the liver.

Separate the 2 lobes of the liver by pulling apart and then cutting with a sharp knife. Remove any green gall spots (rare).

Using a sharp knife, scrape off the fine skin that covers the liver.

Split the larger lobe in half lengthwise and remove the large central vein by pulling and cutting away.

Pull away the vein that runs into the smaller lobe.

Cut away as many blood spots as possible while trying to keep the lobes as intact as possible.

Place the cleaned liver sections in a bowl and season the lobes evenly with the ingredients according to the weight of the liver. Cover and refrigerate 10-12 hours, turning once or twice.

*Preheat the oven to 250 degrees.*

Then place the marinated *foie gras* sections into a small ovenproof terrine, approximately 6-inches x 4-inches x 3-inches high. Press them together slightly to shape and eliminate air pockets. Cover with parchment paper.

Place the terrine in a larger pan and fill with warm tap water halfway up the sides of the terrine. Place in the oven and bake until the internal temperature of the terrine reaches 135 degrees, approximately 1 hour and 15 minutes. Use a meat thermometer to verify.

Remove the terrine from the water bath and allow to cool for 2 hours. The terrine should be weighted in order to keep the loaf compact and thereby facilitate slicing. Cover the terrine with fresh parchment paper and place another terrine on top. A 10-ounce can will serve as the weight.

Refrigerate overnight before removing the pâté from the mold.

## TO SERVE:

Dip a sharp knife in hot water to aid slicing. Serve with toasted slices of country bread.

*Hint:* As there are no preservatives and the liver is about medium, the terrine should be consumed within 2 days. Only duck *foie gras* is available fresh in the United States.

# Soufflés of Lobster with Kohlrabi Purée

*This modern version has the soufflé baked right in the lobster shell. Kohlrabi is a member of the cabbage family whose fleshy stalk resembles a turnip. Tender when young, kohlrabi is available in autumn and is often prepared like turnip, celeriac, and root vegetables in general.*

THE MOUSSE:

> 4 ounces firm white fish fillet: rockfish, seabass, etc.
> 1 medium egg
> $^1/_3$ cup heavy whipping cream
> $^1/_2$ teaspoon Cognac
> $^1/_2$ teaspoon finely chopped dill
> Sea salt
> Freshly ground pepper
> Pinch of cayenne pepper
> 2 quarts Aromatic Broth (page 237)
> 1 2-pound lobster

THE PURÉE:

> 2 cups water
> $^1/_2$ cup sliced onions
> 2 tablespoons diced white of leek, carefully washed
> $^1/_2$ teaspoon sea salt
> $^1/_2$ pound kohlrabi, peeled
> 1 teaspoon butter (optional)
> $^1/_3$ cup heavy whipping cream
> Pinch of nutmeg
> Sea salt
> Freshly ground pepper
> $^1/_4$ cup White Butter Sauce (page 233)

## TO PREPARE THE FISH MOUSSE:

Remove any bones or skin that might remain on the fish. Cut the fish into 1-inch pieces and place in the bowl of a food processor. Purée the fish in the food processor fitted with a steel blade.

152

With the processor running, add the egg and process until the egg is completely blended into the fish. Slowly pour in the heavy cream (with machine running) until completely incorporated. Add the remaining ingredients and give the mousse a final spin to blend. Poach a small amount of the mousse in lightly salted water and taste. Adjust seasonings, if necessary. Chill completely.

Prepare the Aromatic Broth.

Plunge the lobster in the boiling Aromatic Broth. When the broth returns to a rolling boil, remove from heat. Remove the lobster from the broth and allow the lobster to cool.

Separate the claws from the body and split the body in half lengthwise.

Remove the meat from the lobster by cracking the claws and pulling out the tail meat. Cut all the meat into bite-sized pieces.

Store the lobster meat in some cooled broth and refrigerate, if not using immediately.

Rinse the lobster shell halves under cold running water and drain well. Reserve.

## TO PREPARE THE PURÉE:

Combine the water, onion, leek, and salt in a small saucepan. Place over high heat and bring to a boil. Reduce heat and simmer for 5 minutes, until the vegetables are somewhat tender. Slice the kohlrabi into $1/2$-inch thick pieces and add to the saucepan. Cover and boil gently for about 12-15 minutes until the thickest piece can easily be pierced with a fork. Most of the water should have evaporated.

Purée the kohlrabi mixture in a food processor. Return the purée to the saucepan and add the butter, cream, nutmeg, salt, and pepper. Reheat and adjust seasonings.

*Hint:* Do not purée the mixture too finely; some small vegetable chunks make for a more pleasing texture.

The butter and cream may be omitted and replaced with a little olive oil.

## TO ASSEMBLE THE SOUFFLÉS:

*Preheat the oven to 400 degrees.*

Up to 1 hour before serving, divide the prepared lobster meat between the split lobster halves, filling head and tail.

With the aid of a small spatula, cover the meat with the mousse, approximately $1/2$-inch thick.

Place the prepared lobster halves on a small sheet pan.

Bake in the preheated oven for about 10-12 minutes until the mousse is golden brown.

Serve immediately with White Butter Sauce and kohlrabi purée.

# Fillets of Sole with Oysters and Alsatian Crémant Sauce

*This erotic dish has four of the most sensuous foods in the world, sole, oysters, caviar, and champagne. Crémant is a term used for sparkling wine outside of the Champagne region, especially in Alsace.*

> 1/2 cup each: julienne leeks, carrots, and celery root
> 4 fillets of sole (lemon or gray sole), deboned and skinned
> Sea salt
> Freshly ground pepper
> 1 teaspoon butter
> 1/2 teaspoon finely minced shallots
> 1/2 cup crémant or champagne
> 6-8 shucked medium-sized oysters
> 1/2 cup heavy whipping cream
> 1 ounce osetra caviar or salmon roe
> Sprig of fresh dill

## TO PREPARE THE FISH:

Clean, peel, and cut the vegetables into a matchstick-size julienne and steam or parboil in salted water for 1-2 minutes. Julienne should be *al dente*. Immediately plunge into cold water, drain, and reserve.

Lay the prepared sole fillets, white side down, on your work surface. Season lightly with sea salt and pepper. Divide the vegetables into 4 portions and place each bundle on the large end of a fillet. Fold the end of the sole fillet over the vegetable bundle in jelly-roll fashion. Place each folded side down in a small saucepan smeared with the butter and the minced shallots. Season the fillets with sea salt and freshly ground pepper. Pour the champagne around the fish and place the pan over high heat. Bring to a boil, cover, and boil for about 3 minutes until the fillets are just cooked through.

Remove pan from heat, lift the fillets out of the pan onto a dish, and keep warm by placing over a pot of simmering water.

Place the pan in which the fillets were cooked back on high heat and add the oysters. Lift the oysters out of the wine with a slotted spoon as soon as the liquid begins to boil again. Keep warm with the fillets.

## TO PREPARE THE SAUCE:

Boil the wine over high heat until reduced by two-thirds, about 2 minutes. Add the cream and boil for another 2 minutes to thicken until the sauce is thick enough to coat a spoon. Remove from heat, taste, and adjust seasonings.

## TO ASSEMBLE:

Divide the sole fillets and oysters onto two serving plates. Coat with the sauce and garnish the oysters with the caviar.

Add the sprig of dill and serve.

# Roasted Salmon "Larded" with Foie Gras and Truffles

*A special tool, a "larding needle," is used to insert the foie gras and truffles. This tool consists of a hollow stainless steel skewer, pointed at one end and with the other slotted in a wooden or metal handle. In this elegant preparation, the enticing flavors of truffles and foie gras seduce the senses.*

THE LENTILS:

    2 cups of water
    ¹/₂ cup green or red lentils
    2-inch piece of celery
    2-inch piece of carrot
    2 tablespoons chopped onion
    2 cloves
    1 bay leaf
    Sea salt
    Freshly ground pepper

THE LENTIL CASSOULET:

    2 tablespoons diced bacon
    2 tablespoons finely chopped onion
    ¹/₂ cup dry white wine
    1 tablespoon diced cooked tomato
    ¹/₂ teaspoon finely chopped garlic
    Reserved diced vegetables
    Reserved lentil cooking liquid
    ¹/₂ cup White Stock (page 228)

THE GARNISH:

    8 pearl onions
    6 baby carrots
    6 baby turnips

THE SALMON:

    2 4-ounce salmon fillets
    1 ounce *foie gras*
    1 ounce fresh truffle
    ¹/₂ teaspoon Pâté Spices (page 228)
    Sea salt
    Freshly ground pepper

### TO COOK THE LENTILS:

Place the water, celery, carrot, onion, cloves, bay leaf, salt, and pepper in a saucepan and bring to a boil. Simmer 10 minutes and add the lentils. Cover the pan and boil for 20 minutes until the lentils are tender.

Remove and reserve the carrot and celery. Drain the lentils, reserving the cooking liquid.

### TO PREPARE THE LENTIL CASSOULET:

In a heavy-bottomed saucepan, heat the diced bacon and sauté for 1 minute. Add the chopped onion and sauté 1-2 minutes until lightly browned. Add the white wine and bring to a boil. Pour in the reserved cooking liquid (about ½ cup) and add the tomato and garlic.

Bring to a boil and reduce by a third. While the liquid is reducing, dice the reserved carrot and celery and add to the liquid. Add the cooked lentils to the reduced liquid, bring to a boil and remove from heat. Taste and adjust seasonings.

The lentils should be somewhat "soupy" because they act as a sauce for this dish. If too thick add some White Stock to dilute.

### TO PREPARE GARNISHES:

Trim and peel the baby vegetables. Steam lightly and sauté in butter. Season with sea salt and pepper.

### TO PREPARE THE SALMON:

*Preheat the oven to 425 degrees.*

Cut the *foie gras* into 4½ x ½ x 1-inch strips (approximately).

Cut the truffle into 4½ x ½ x 1-inch strips (approximately).

With the aid of a larding needle, "lard" each salmon fillet with 2 pieces of truffle and 2 pieces of *foie gras*.

Season the salmon with the pâté spices, salt, and pepper.

Place salmon on a lightly oiled baking sheet and bake in the oven for approximately 8-10 minutes until just cooked through.

### TO SERVE:

Place 3-4 tablespoons of the lentil cassouet in the center of a warm plate. Top with the salmon fillet and garnish with the assorted glazed baby root vegetables. Serve remaining lentils on the side.

# Frog Leg Mousseline

*Visit Alsace and you will see the large storks nests built around village towers. The birds return to Alsace each year because of the abundance of frogs, one of the stork's principal foods. Watercress is a member of the mustard family that grows partially submerged in water.*

THE MOUSSE:

> 5 ounces of pike, sole or other firm white fish
> 1 medium egg
> $\frac{1}{2}$ cup heavy whipping cream
> Sea salt
> Freshly ground pepper
> 2 6-ounce ramekins
> 1 tablespoon butter

THE FROG LEGS AND SAUCE:

> $\frac{1}{2}$ pound of frog legs (4 large pairs)
> 2 teaspoons butter
> 1 teaspoon finely minced shallots
> $\frac{2}{3}$ cup Alsatian wine, Riesling, or Pinot Blanc
> $\frac{1}{2}$ cup heavy whipping cream
> Sea salt
> Freshly ground pepper
> $\frac{1}{2}$ teaspoon lemon juice
> 1 tablespoon finely chopped watercress

## TO PREPARE THE MOUSSE:

Cut the pike into small pieces. Place the fish in the bowl of a food processor fitted with the steel blade. Process for 1 minute to purée. With the processor running, add the egg, salt, and pepper, blending thoroughly. Slowly pour in the heavy cream until completely incorporated.

Poach a small amount of mousse in lightly salted water, taste and adjust seasonings, if necessary. Refrigerate mousse for at least 1 hour.

## TO PREPARE THE MOLDS:

Generously butter the two oven-proof ramekins. Fill the two ramekins with the chilled mousse. With a tablespoon, hollow out the mousse from the center of the ramekin, forming a "nest." The coating should be approximately $\frac{1}{2}$-inch thick all around. Refrigerate ramekins and remaining mousse.

## TO PREPARE THE FROG LEGS AND SAUCE:

Melt the 2 teaspoons of butter in a small saucepan, add the minced shallots, the frog legs, and the white wine.

Season with salt and pepper and bring to a boil over high heat.

Reduce flame and simmer gently for about 4 minutes for large frog legs until they are just cooked through. Remove pan from heat.

Using a slotted spoon, remove the frog legs from the pan and set on a plate to cool. Remove as much of the meat from the bones as possible, refrigerate, and cool completely.

Return liquid in the pan to a boil and reduce cooking liquid by half (about 4 minutes). Add the heavy cream and return to a boil. Reduce the volume of cream by a third and remove from heat. Add the lemon juice, the chopped watercress, taste, and adjust seasonings. Keep warm.

## TO PREPARE THE MOUSSELINES:

*Preheat oven to 425 degrees.*

Fill the mousseline nests with the reserved frog leg meats and pour 1 teaspoon of the sauce over them. Reserve any remaining meats to garnish the plates.

Cover the nests with the remaining mousse, completely encasing the filling.

Place the filled ramekins in a shallow baking dish. Fill the dish half full with warm water, set on the stove, and bring to a boil over high heat. Transfer the pan to the oven and bake in preheated oven until the mousse just begins to brown, about 12 minutes. Remove from the oven and lift the ramekins out of the water bath. Allow ramekins to rest a few minutes before unmolding.

## TO SERVE:

Unmold by inverting into the center of individual ovenproof plates. Garnish each plate with ½ of any of the remaining frog leg meats. Place the plates in the oven for a few minutes to heat. Coat each mousseline with the warm sauce and serve at once.

Garnish with watercress.

*Variation:* Stuff the mousseline with crabmeat.

# Fillets of Sole with Truffles

*There is a famous saying about truffles: "Those who wish to lead virtuous lives should abstain". On the other hand, without a little vice, can there be virtue?*

> 1 ounce of truffle
> 1 large shiitake mushroom
> 6 fillets of lemon or Dover sole (approximately ¹/₂ pound)
> Sea salt
> Freshly ground pepper
> 1 tablespoon butter
> ¹/₂ teaspoon finely minced shallots
> ¹/₂ cup dry white wine
> ¹/₂ cup heavy whipping cream
> 1 medium egg
> ¹/₄ stick butter

Wash and brush the truffles, if raw. Peel the truffles, reserving the peelings for another use such as Truffle Ice Cream (page 194). Cut the truffles into a fine julienne and set aside.

Wash the shiitake mushroom and remove the stem (may be reserved for making a stock). Cut the mushroom into a fine julienne.

Trim any dark outer or translucent gray inner skin from the fillets. Place the sole fillets, white side down, on your work surface. Season lightly with salt and pepper and fold each in half, lengthwise. (Place a slice or 2 of truffle on the lower half of the fillets before folding, if desired.)

Butter a flameproof casserole or small saucepan just large enough to accommodate the fillets and sprinkle with the shallots. Arrange the sole fillets in the casserole and sprinkle with the julienne of truffles and mushroom, salt, and pepper.

Whip the heavy cream and reserve.

*Preheat the broiler.*

Pour the white wine over the sole fillets and bring to a boil over high heat. Reduce heat, cover, and simmer gently for about 2¹/₂ minutes, or until the fillets are just cooked through.

Remove from the heat and strain the cooking liquid into a small heavy saucepan. Bring to boil over high heat and reduce by half. Transfer fish to an ovenproof serving platter, dividing the julienne truffle and mushroom over the fillets. Cover fish and keep warm (see hint).

While the liquid is reducing, place the egg in a small mixing bowl and beat thoroughly, forming a mock hollandise.

Melt the butter and pour into egg, beating constantly. Set aside.

When the poaching liquid is reduced, remove from heat. Whisk the egg and butter mixture into the hot reduced liquid.

Gently fold the whipped cream into the pan.

Taste and adjust seasonings.

Coat the fillets with the sauce. Place under the broiler and brown lightly.

Serve immediately.

*Hint:* Keep the fish warm while preparing the sauce by leaving a small amount of the cooking liquid in the bottom of the pan and covering the fish with a damp towel. Set the pan in a 200-degree oven or leave the door open if the oven is hot. The fish will remain warm and moist without over-cooking for about 15 minutes.

Placing the covered fish over a pot of barely simmering water is another way to hold the fish while preparing the sauce.

Assigning a specific cooking time for fish is difficult. Fish is done when slightly firm and springy to the touch. Another test is to place a knife or narrow spatula under the fillet and lift it to expose the center. Remove the fish just as the center turns from translucent to opaque.

# Grouper Marseillaise

*Saffron is the dried stigmas of the crocus and costs about $800 a pound today, making it the world's most expensive spice. The hand-picked stigmas of 4,000 blossoms are required to produce one ounce of saffron. Fortunately, a little goes a long way.*

12 ounces grouper fillet
½ tablespoon finely chopped shallots
½ teaspoon finely chopped garlic
2 tablespoons chopped tomato
½ cup dry white wine
½ teaspoon saffron
Sea salt
Freshly ground pepper
3 ounces Hollandaise Sauce (page 242)
½ teaspoon Pernod, anise flavored beverage

Cut the grouper into 2 portions and salt and pepper the filets.

Place the shallots, garlic, tomato, white wine, and saffron in a medium saucepan. Add the prepared grouper fillets and place over high heat. Bring to a boil, reduce heat, and cover. Boil gently until the fish is just cooked through, approximately 4-5 minutes.

Transfer fish from the pan with a slotted spatula, place on a serving platter, and cover to prevent the fish from drying.

Keep warm by placing over a pan of simmering water.

Place the saucepan containing the broth over high heat, bring the liquid to a boil, and reduce by half, approximately 2 minutes. Remove pan from flame.

Allow the pan to cool for 1-2 minutes, then add the Pernod and Hollandaise, whisking thoroughly. Taste and adjust seasonings.

If the fish has cooled, place the covered fish in a 350-degree oven for about 2 minutes to warm.

Pour any juices from the fish platter into the saucepan, stir the sauce and coat the grouper fillets.

Serve with boiled potatoes or Brown Rice Pilaf (page 51).

*Variation:* Those who do not wish to prepare a Hollandaise Sauce may whisk an equal amount of butter into the sauce.

# Lobster with Whiskey Sauce and Purée Rose

*This intoxicating presentation is certain to knock-em out. This root vegetable purée has a stunning rose color. Russian peasants kept their cheeks rosy by using beets as home-grown rouge.*

THE PURÉE:

> $1/2$ pound celery root (1 cup)
> $1/2$ pound potato (1 cup)
> $1/2$ pound beet (1 cup)
> 1 tablespoon finely chopped onion
> 1 tablespoon butter
> 1 tablespoon heavy whipping cream
> Sea salt
> Freshly ground pepper

THE LOBSTERS:

> 2 $1^1/_2$-pound lobsters or 1 2-3-pound lobster
> 2 tablespoons olive oil
> 2 tablespoons bourbon
> 1 cup dry white wine or champagne
> 2 teaspoons finely chopped shallots
> $1/2$ teaspoon finely chopped garlic
> 2 tablespoons tomato purée

THE SAUCE:

> 2 tablespoons softened butter
> $2/_3$ cup heavy whipping cream
> Pinch of cayenne pepper
> Sea salt
> Freshly ground pepper
> 2-3 teaspoons bourbon
> 1 teaspoon finely chopped parsley

## TO PREPARE THE PURÉE:

Peel the celery root, potato, and beet. Dice each, keeping them separate.

Bring $2/_3$ cup of salted water to a boil in a heavy bottomed saucepan. Add the diced beets and chopped onion, cover and boil for 10 minutes.

Add the celery root and potato and stir; do not recover the pan. Cook until the celery root is tender, approximately 15 minutes.

Test pieces of celery root for doneness.

Place contents of saucepan in a food processor fitted with the steel blade and process until very smooth. Add the butter and heavy cream, process for 10 seconds. Taste and adjust seasonings.

*Hint:* May be prepared ahead and reheated. Adding a few drops of red wine vinegar to the purée heightens the flavor.

## TO PREPARE THE LOBSTERS:

Using a sharp heavy knife with the blade pointed in the direction of the lobster's eyes, force the point of the knife into the base of the head just above the joint between the tail and head of the lobster; then cut down through the center of the head between the eyes, splitting it in half. Cut away the head from the tail. Remove and discard the stomach sac behind the eyes. Remove the tomalley and coral and reserve in a small bowl. Cut the lobster tails into 3 medallions each. Remove the claws and crack them with the blunt edge of the blade. Cut the split lobster head into several large pieces. Reserve as much lobster juice as possible by scraping the cutting board.

Heat the olive oil in a large saucepan over high flame. When the olive oil just begins to smoke, add the lobster claws, medallions, and pieces of the lobster head.

Sauté 2 minutes, tossing often, until the claws and medallions redden; cover and cook another 2 minutes, tossing once or twice.

Add the bourbon and flame. Return pan to high heat and deglaze with the white wine. Add the shallots, garlic, tomato paste, and cayenne; bring to a boil, reduce heat, cover, and simmer for about 2 minutes until the lobster claws and medallions are cooked.

Remove lobster medallions and claws from the sauté pan and place on a platter, cover, and set aside.

## TO PREPARE THE SAUCE:

Allow the pieces of the head to remain. Add heavy whipping cream and boil uncovered for another 3-4 minutes to reduce liquid.

While the lobster sauce is simmering, thoroughly whisk the softened butter and the reserved tomalley and coral.

Remove the pieces of lobster head with a slotted spoon.

Whisk the butter/tomalley mixture into the reduced liquid to thicken. Bring to a boil and remove from heat, add the remaining bourbon, taste and adjust seasonings.

Remove the meat from the lobster claws and medallions and place in the pan of warm sauce to heat. Arrange the lobster meats on a warm platter.

Coat the lobster with the warm sauce, sprinkle with chopped parsley, and serve immediately.

Serve with the Purée Rose.

*Hint:* Using the 1 larger rather than 2 smaller lobsters will increase the cooking time.

# Fillets of Sole with Caviar

*Caviar is a symbol of elegance, perhaps the most highly regarded love food. Its reputation as an aphrodisiac may also have to do with the many vitamins and sea minerals it contains. A series of studies in Japan noted that seafood eaters were much less likely to die of strokes. Researchers theorize that the omega-3 fatty acids in seafood may modify blood factors, helping protect against stroke.*

> 6 fillets of lemon or grey sole (approximately 1/2 pound)
> Sea salt
> Freshly ground pepper
> 1 tablespoon butter
> 1/2 teaspoon finely minced shallots
> 1/2 cup dry white wine
> 1/3 cup heavy whipping cream
> 1 ounce of caviar

Trim any dark outer or translucent gray inner skin from the fillets. Place the sole fillets, white side down, on your work surface. Season lightly with salt and pepper and fold each in half, lengthwise.

Butter a flameproof casserole or small saucepan just large enough to accommodate the fillets and sprinkle with the shallots. Arrange the sole fillets in the casserole and season with salt and pepper.

Pour the white wine over the sole fillets and bring to a boil over high heat. Reduce heat, cover, and simmer gently for about 2 1/2 minutes, or until the fillets are just cooked through.

Remove from the heat and strain the cooking liquid into a small heavy saucepan. Bring to boil over high heat and reduce by half. Transfer fish to an ovenproof serving platter. Cover fish and keep warm (see hint).

When the liquid is reduced, add the heavy cream and return to a boil. Reduce the cream by half and remove from heat.

Gently stir in 1/2 of the caviar and taste and adjust seasonings.

Coat the fillets with the sauce.

Serve immediately. Garnish with a dollop of the remaining caviar.

*Hint:* Keep the fish warm while preparing the sauce by leaving a small amount of the cooking liquid in the bottom of the pan and covering the fish with a damp towel. Set the pan in a 200-degree oven or leave the door open if the oven is hot. The fish will remain warm and moist without over-cooking for about 15 minutes.

Placing the covered fish over a pot of barely simmering water is another way to hold the fish while preparing the sauce.

Assigning a specific cooking time for fish is difficult. Fish is done when slightly firm and springy to the touch. Another test is to place a knife or narrow spatula under the fillet and lift it to expose the center. Remove the fish just as the center turns from translucent to opaque.

*Variation:* Use Dover sole.

# Lobster with Sauternes Sauce

*Who could forget the dinner scene from the movie, "Tom Jones," in which the couple work themselves up to a frenzy supping on lobster and oysters. Sauternes is the famous white-wine region south of the city of Bordeaux. Due to its location, the grapes can be affected in some years by "noble rot." This acts on the ripe and eventually overripe fruit and concentrates the juice in each grape. These grapes must be hand-picked often one at a time. The resulting wine is rich, very fragrant and luscious, with high sugar.*

> 1 quart Aromatic Broth (see page 237)
> 2 1-pound Maine lobsters
> 1 cup Sauternes (drink the remaining wine while preparing sauce)
> 2 tablespoons heavy whipping cream
> 1 stick of butter
> Sea salt
> Freshly ground pepper
> 1/4 teaspoon finely chopped fresh ginger
> 1 orange
> 1 grapefruit
> 1 papaya or mango

Bring the Aromatic Broth to a rolling boil and add the lobsters. As soon as the liquid returns to a boil, remove the lobsters from the broth. When the lobsters are cool enough to handle, remove the meat by splitting the lobsters in half lengthwise. Use the blunt side of a heavy knife to crack open the claws. Store the lobster meat by covering with some of the broth and reserving in the refrigerator. Use the lobster shells and remaining broth to prepare a Lobster Bisque or Sauce (page 236).

Section the orange and the grapefruit. The dish requires 2 or 3 citrus sections per person. Peel and dice the mango or papaya. Set aside.

## TO PREPARE THE SAUCE:

Allow the butter to soften slightly. Place the Sauternes or late harvest wine in a small saucepan over high heat. Reduce the wine by half. Add the cream and bring to a boil. Reduce heat to the lowest setting. Whisk in the butter, several pieces at a time. Whisk constantly until all the butter has been incorporated into the sauce and remove from heat. Add ginger, taste, and adjust seasonings. Sauce may be held by placing in a double boiler filled with hot tap water.

Drain the lobster and bring the broth it was stored in to a boil. Warm two plates in a low oven. Place several citrus sections in each plate as well as a tablespoon of the diced tropical fruit. Plunge the reserved lobster meat in the hot broth for 15-20 seconds. Remove with a slotted spoon and arrange on the warm, garnished plates. Spoon the sauce over the lobster and serve immediately.

*Variation:* Use other sweet or late harvest wines for the sauce. The cream in the sauce may be omitted.

# Poached Turbot with Celery Root Purée and Sauce Maltaise

*Maltaise is the name given to any sweet or savory sauce based on oranges, particularly the Maltese blood orange. Turbot is one of the most highly regarded saltwater fish. Its delicate white firm flaky flesh seems best suited for poaching or baking. Celery root or celeriac is a root vegetable with a nobby turnip-like shape and celery-like flavor. The stalks, though usually not eaten, are used to flavor soups or stocks much like celery.*

1 1-1½ pound Turbot

THE BROTH:

⅓ cup each: julienned celery, carrots
⅓ cup julienned leeks, carefully washed to remove all grit
⅓ cup finely shredded onions
2 cups water
⅓ cup dry white wine
1 tablespoon red wine vinegar
1 teaspoon sea salt
Pinch of freshly ground pepper
1 *bouquet garni* consisting of 1 bay leaf, 2 cloves, ½ teaspoon
    cracked peppercorns, pinch of thyme, ½ teaspoon coriander
    seeds, wrapped in cheesecloth

THE CELERY ROOT PURÉE:

2 cups water
½ cup sliced onions
2 tablespoons diced white of leek, thoroughly washed to remove
    all sand
½ pound peeled celery root
1 teaspoon butter, optional
⅓ cup heavy whipping cream
Pinch of nutmeg
Sea salt
Freshly ground pepper

THE SAUCE MALTAISE:

For ½ cup

> 1 stick butter
> 2 egg yolks
> 1 tablespoon warm water
> Pinch of sea salt
> Dash of cayenne pepper
> ⅓ cup freshly squeezed blood orange juice
> ½ teaspoon of orange zest

## TO PREPARE THE BROTH:

Combine all of the broth ingredients in a heavy saucepan and place over high heat. Bring to a boil; lower the heat and simmer for 30 minutes. Taste and adjust seasonings. The broth should taste a little too strong, as poaching the fish will dilute the strength.

## TO PREPARE THE CELERY ROOT PURÉE:

Combine the water, onion, leek, and salt in a small saucepan.

Place over high heat and bring to a boil. Reduce heat and simmer for 5 minutes, until the vegetables are somewhat tender. Slice the celery root into ½-inch thick pieces and add to the saucepan. Cover and boil gently for about 12-15 minutes until the thickest piece can easily be pierced with a fork. Most of the water should have evaporated.

Purée the contents of the pan in a food processor. Return the purée to the saucepan and add the butter, cream, nutmeg, salt, and pepper. Reheat and adjust seasonings.

*Hint:* Do not purée the mixture too finely; some small vegetable chunks make for a more pleasing texture.

The butter and cream may be omitted and replaced with a little olive oil.

## TO PREPARE THE SAUCE:

Melt the butter over low heat. Clarify by skimming off the foam and carefully pouring off the butter, leaving the milky residue in the bottom of the pan.

In a small stainless steel or glass bowl, whip together the egg yolks and tablespoon of warm water with a whisk until smooth. Avoid aluminum as it discolors the yolks.

Place the bowl over a pan of simmering water to form a double boiler. Beat continuously, using the whisk to scrape the mixture from the bottom and sides of the bowl. Beating vigorously in a figure-8 pattern incorporates more air, and thereby results in a lighter sauce. Season with salt, pepper, and cayenne pepper.

### TO FINISH THE SAUCE:

Place the orange juice in a small pan over high heat, bring to boil and reduce by half. Remove from heat and allow to cool to lukewarm. Whisk into the hollandaise along with the orange zest. Taste and adjust seasonings.

*Hint:* Blood oranges are usually only found around the holidays and into the winter months. Substitute whatever oranges are in season. It is not absolutely necessary to reduce the orange juice, merely add a little at a time until the desired taste is achieved.

### TO PREPARE THE FISH:

Remove the head with a sharp heavy knife and split the fish by cutting down the length of the turbot on either side of the spine. Rinse the sections under cold running water.

### TO POACH THE TURBOT:

Place the turbot sections in the simmering broth. Begin timing the fish when the broth returns to a boil; pieces 1-inch thick will cook in approximately 10 minutes. As one side of the turbot is larger, each section may have different cooking times.

Lift the cooked section out of the broth and place on a large platter or small sheet pan.

Using a fork, carefully scrape the dark skin off the top of the fish section. Slide the fork between the layer of bones that runs vertically through the section. Lift off the top piece of fillet, keeping it as intact as possible. Pull off the bones, flip the lower fillet over, and scrape off the skin.

### TO SERVE:

Arrange the fillets in two large warm shallow bowls.

Ladle about 2 ounces of the broth with vegetables over the fish. Serve with the Sauce Maltaise and Celery Root Purée.

# Quail Stuffed with Foie Gras

*Let me warn you that eating game may bring out the wild streak we all have inside us. Be prepared should a little wildness ensue. We really are what we eat.*

THE QUAIL:

      4 partially boneless quail
      Sea salt
      Freshly ground pepper
      2 tablespoons butter
      1 tablespoon oil
      1 cup Chicken Sauce (page 45)

THE STUFFING:

      3 ounces duck meat (substitute chicken breast)
      3 ounces fresh *foie gras*
      1/2 teaspoon salt
      Pinch of freshly ground pepper
      Pinch of Pâté Spices (page 228)
      1 whole egg
      1/2 cup heavy whipping cream
      1 1/2 teaspoons Cognac

## TO PREPARE THE STUFFING:

Cut the duck meat and *foie gras* into small pieces and finely grind in a food processor fitted with the steel blade. Add the seasonings and egg, blending thoroughly. Slowly pour the cream through the feed tube with the motor running until completely incorporated. Taste for seasonings and chill.

## TO PREPARE THE QUAIL:

Use a piece of kitchen twine to tie off the neck opening and season the inside of each quail with a little salt and pepper. Fill a pastry bag with the prepared meat and stuff the quail, dividing the stuffing evenly among the 4 birds. Bend the legs forward against the body and tie securely, completely enclosing the quail cavity.

*Preheat oven to 400 degrees.*

Melt the butter and oil in a heavy skillet over high heat. When the butter begins to brown, place the quail in the pan and sear lightly on all sides. Place in the oven and roast for 18 minutes until the stuffing is completely cooked through. Remove the quail from the oven and cut away the string. Set quail aside and keep warm.

## TO PREPARE THE SAUCE:

Pour the grease from skillet and add the Chicken Stock. Bring to a boil and scrape the bottom of the pan. Transfer the liquid to a small saucepan. Boil again, skim thoroughly, and remove from the heat.

Taste and adjust seasonings.

## TO SERVE:

Place 2 quail per person on warm plates. Divide the sauce evenly. Serve with wild rice and seasonal vegetables such as corn.

# Medallions of Texas Antelope with Roebuck Sauce and Root Vegetable Gratin

*The horns of male antelopes represent strength and dominance. Males with the biggest, most impressive horns usually attract a mate. The Negril antelope was introduced into Texas from India and is one of the only true wild game available to restaurants.*

THE ROEBUCK SAUCE:

> 1 tablespoon butter
> 1 tablespoon finely chopped onion
> 1 tablespoon finely diced country ham
> 1/4 cup dry white wine
> 2 tablespoons red wine vinegar
> 1/2 cup basic Deer Sauce (page 230)
> 2 teaspoons red currant jelly
> Sea salt
> Freshly ground pepper

THE GRATIN:

> 1/4 pound yukon gold potatoes
> 1/4 pound carrots
> 1/4 pound turnips
> 1/2 cup heavy whipping cream
> 2 ounces grated Parmesan cheese
> 1 tablespoon butter
> 1/3 teaspoon finely minced garlic
> Sea salt
> Freshly ground pepper

THE ANTELOPE:

> 10-12 ounces antelope loin
> Sea salt
> 1 tablespoon olive oil
> 1 tablespoon butter

*Bouillabaisse (page 108)*

*Wild Mushroom Napoleon (page 143)*

*Warm Chocolate Tart*
(page 130)

Quail Stuffed with Foie Gras
(page 174)

Beef Rib in a Salt Crust (page 180)

*Rack of Lamb (page 182)*

*Beef Wellington (page 188)*

*Tartare of Arctic Char (page 207)*

*Baked Alaska (page 195)*

*Wild Duck Salad (page 218)*

Trio of Mousses: Izarra Mousse, (page 224)
Cinnamon Mousse (page 58) and
Espresso Mousse (page 19)

## TO PREPARE THE SAUCE:

Heat the butter in a small saucepan. Just as the butter begins to brown, add the onions and simmer for 3-4 minutes until translucent. Add the ham, stir well, and cook for 1 minute.

Add the wine and vinegar, increase heat, and reduce liquid until almost dry.

Add the Deer Sauce, bring to a boil, reduce heat, and simmer about 10 minutes. Whisk in the currant jelly and season with salt and pepper.

## TO PREPARE THE GRATIN:

*Preheat oven to 400 degrees.*

Peel the potato, carrot, and turnip. Thinly slice.

Blanch the root vegetables by dropping in lighly salted boiling water for approximately 1-2 minutes. Drain thoroughly and pat dry in a towel. Place the vegetables in a mixing bowl and add the garlic, salt, and pepper; toss.

Butter the bottom and sides of a small baking dish, place $^1/_2$ the vegetables in a layer and cover with $^1/_2$ of the grated cheese. Cover with the remaining vegetables. Pour the heavy cream over the vegetables and cover with the remaining cheese. Dot the top with the remaining butter.

Cover the dish and place in a preheated oven for 15 minutes. Remove the cover and allow approximately 5-8 more minutes in the oven to brown the cheese.

## TO PREPARE THE ANTELOPE:

Trim excess fat and silver skin from the loin. Slice the loin into 4 medallions, approximately $^1/_2$-inch thick. Season the medallions with salt and pepper.

Place a skillet large enough to hold the medallions over high heat and add the olive oil and butter. When the butter just begins to brown, add the meat and quickly sear.

Sear for about 1 minute per side, browning nicely.

## TO SERVE:

Transfer the medallions to serving plates and pour the warm sauce around the meat. Garnish with root vegetable gratin.

*Variation:* Substitute basic Veal or Beef Sauce (page 232) for the Deer Stock. Substitute native deer for the antelope.

# Châteaubriand with Béarnaise Sauce and Sautéed Potatoes with Scallions

*This luxurious meal was named in honor of the French writer and bon vivant, Vicomte François René Châteaubriand, who passed on at the age of eighty in the arms of his young mistress.*

THE POTATOES:

> ½ pound Yukon Gold potatoes (approximately 2 medium)
> 1½ tablespoons olive oil or rendered duck fat
> 1 tablespoon butter
> 2 scallions, finely minced
> Sea salt
> Freshly ground pepper

THE MEAT:

> 1 18-20-ounce center cut of beef tenderloin
> 1 teaspoon sea salt
> 1 teaspoon cracked black peppercorns
> 1 tablespoon butter
> 1 tablespoon oil
> Béarnaise Sauce (page 243)

## TO PREPARE THE POTATOES:

Wash potatoes. Place unpeeled in a 1-quart saucepan and cover with cold water. Bring to a boil, reduce heat, and simmer about 15 minutes. Potatoes must be only partly cooked. Test for doneness by piercing potatoes with a large meat fork. The fork should meet with some resistance; cool the potatoes under cold running water.

Peel the potatoes, cut them in half, and then into slices ½-inch thick

Heat the oil and butter in a heavy skillet. When the butter begins to brown, add the potato slices. Cook the potatoes until well browned and crisp, tossing frequently, approximately 5 minutes.

Add the scallions and a pinch of salt and pepper. Toss and keep warm.

## TO PREPARE THE BEEF:

Trim any fat and silver skin that covers the meat. Place the meat, large end up, in the center of a dish towel. Wrap the towel tightly around the meat. Gather the loose ends of the towel and grasp firmly to securely hold the meat upright.

Pound the "Château" with the flat side of a meat cleaver to approximately half of the original height. The flatter and more cylindrical the shape, the easier it is to cook and slice the meat.

Season the meat with salt and cracked black peppercorns. Heat the butter and oil in a heavy skillet over high heat. When the butter browns, sear the meat well on both sides. Lower the flame slightly and cook the meat a total of 16 minutes for medium rare. Using tongs, turn the meat several times to ensure even cooking. Do not use forks.

## TO SERVE:

*Preheat oven to 375 degrees.*

Remove the meat from the pan and let it rest 5-10 minutes before finishing. Arrange the potatoes in clusters around the sides of a large ovenproof platter. Carve the meat on a slant into ³/₈-inch slices and arrange down the center of the platter. Place the prepared platter in the oven for 2-3 minutes to heat. Serve with the Béarnaise Sauce.

*Variation:* Serve the Châteaubriand with any assorted seasonal vegetables such as Baked Tomatoes with Herb Bread Crumbs (page 106).

# Beef Rib Baked in a Salt Crust and Gratin of Spinach and Mushrooms

*Since prehistoric times, salt has been a precious commodity—probably one of the oldest commodities traded by man. The Hebrews used it in sacrifices and ceremonies. Homer described nations as poor when they did not have salt to season their food. The Romans used salt to preserve fish, olives, cheese, and meat and it formed part of the soldiers' wages. In this recipe, I use sea salt (the most nutritious and pure) to form a crust that seals in the juices of the beef and yields an amazing tenderness. I recommend sea salt or unrefined mineral salt. Both contain all the vital trace minerals which are often processed out of ordinary table salt.*

THE GRATIN OF SPINACH AND MUSHROOMS:

> ½ pound spinach
> 4 ounces white mushrooms
> 2 tablespoons butter
> 1 teaspoon finely minced shallots
> ⅔ cup heavy whipping cream
> 1 egg yolk
> ¼ teaspoon of freshly ground nutmeg
> Sea salt
> Freshly ground pepper

THE BEEF:

> 1 16-18 ounce boneless rib-eye
> 1 teaspoon cracked peppercorns
> 1 pound coarse sea or kosher salt
> 4 ounces all-purpose flour
> ¾ cup water

## TO PREPARE THE GRATIN:

Wash several times, de-stem, and thoroughly drain (pat dry) the spinach leaves.

Wash the mushrooms by placing in a large bowl of water. Lift the mushrooms out of the bowl leaving the grit behind.

*Preheat oven to 400 degrees.*

180

Melt 1 tablespoon of butter in a small sauté pan; when the butter begins to foam, add ½ of the shallots; stir into the butter and add the spinach leaves. Cook for approximately 1 minute to just wilt the spinach. Set aside.

Slice the mushrooms.

Wipe the sauté pan clean, melt the remaining tablespoon of butter. When the butter begins to foam, add the remaining shallots; stir into the butter and add the sliced mushrooms. Sauté for 1-2 minutes until just cooked through.

With the aid of a rubber spatula, transfer the mushrooms to a small oven-proof dish. Place the cooked spinach over the mushrooms.

Place the egg yolk in a small mixing bowl and whisk thoroughly. Add the cream, nutmeg, salt, and pepper, blending completely.

Pour the egg/cream combination over the vegetables. Place the dish in a preheated 400-degree oven for 5-7 minutes until nicely browned.

## TO PREPARE THE BEEF:

*Preheat the oven to 500 degrees*

Trim any excess fat and silver skin from the beef.

Season the beef with the cracked peppercorns.

Mix the salt and flour together in a bowl and add the water to obtain a moderately thick paste.

Using the heel of your hand, firmly press the paste around the beef, forming a salt crust.

Place the beef on a baking sheet and place in the preheated oven for approximately 10 minutes. Reduce heat to 450 degrees and bake another 10 minutes for medium-rare. Remove the beef from the oven and allow to rest for 10-12 minutes.

## TO SERVE:

Present the beef and break away the crust with the aid of a large kitchen spoon or spatula.

Place on a cutting board and slice diagonally.

Serve at once with the Gratin of Spinach and Mushrooms and a Madeira Sauce (page 234), if desired.

# Rack of Lamb with Gratin Dauphinois

*Herbs and spices have been considered sexual stimulants since ancient times. In A Midsummer Night's Dream Shakespeare describes a "powerful herb, the juice of which on sleeping eyelids laid will make man or woman madly dote upon the next live creature that it sees." The term, gratin, denotes a method of cooking meat, fish, poultry or vegetables so that a crust forms on the surface while baking in the oven or finished under the broiler. Gratins are usually served in the vessel in which they are baked.*

THE GRATIN:

> 1 large Russet potato
> 1 tablespoon butter
> $\frac{1}{2}$ teaspoon finely minced garlic
> Sea salt
> Freshly ground pepper
> $\frac{1}{2}$ cup heavy whipping cream

THE LAMB:

> 1 rack of lamb
> 1 teaspoon cracked black peppercorns
> Sea salt
> 1 tablespoon vegetable or olive oil
> 1 teaspoon Dijon-style mustard
> 2 tablespoons herb bread crumbs (page 106)
> $\frac{1}{2}$ cup Lamb Sauce (page 230)

*TO PREPARE THE GRATIN:*

Peel, split lengthwise, and thinly slice ($\frac{1}{8}$-inch) the potato.

Approximately 10 ounces of potato should remain.

Do not wash the potato slices.

Smear the butter on the bottom and sides of a shallow ovenproof 2-cup ceramic or pyrex baking dish. Place the potato slices in the baking dish, making several layers.

In a mixing bowl, combine the heavy cream, minced garlic, approximately ½ teaspoon salt, and pinch ground pepper. Taste and adjust seasonings. Pour the mixture over the potato slices. The potatoes must be just covered by the cream; add more cream if necessary.

## TO PREPARE THE LAMB:

*Preheat the oven to 425 degrees.*

Trim rack of lamb, removing excess fat and silver skin. Season the rack with the cracked peppercorns and salt to taste. Heat the oil in a heavy skillet over high heat. When the oil just begins to smoke, sear the meat well on both sides. Set the skillet in the oven. Cook the rack of lamb for approximately 10-12 minutes for medium rare. Using tongs, turn the meat once while in the oven. Remove the lamb from the pan and allow to rest 10 minutes before serving.

## TO SERVE:

Brush the mustard on the front of the rack of lamb and cover with a generous coating of the herb bread crumbs. Return the lamb to a hot oven to heat and brown the bread crumbs, approximately 4-5 minutes. Carve the rack into 6 chops and place in pairs down the center of the serving platter. Present the platter at tableside and serve on warm plates, accompanied by the Lamb Sauce and gratin.

*Variation:* Garnish the rack of lamb with such seasonal vegetables as green beans, grilled onions, carrots, etc.

# Tournedos Rossini with Endives in a Cream Sauce

*Named after the famous composer, this dish combines the power of beef with the erotic glamour of* fois gras *and truffles. Truffles have long been considered powerful aphrodisiacs.*

THE ENDIVE:

    2 large Belgium endives
    Juice of $1/2$ lemon
    1 ounce of butter
    $1/3$ cup heavy whipping cream
    $1/2$ teaspoon paprika
    Sea salt
    Freshly ground pepper

THE BEEF:

    12 ounces beef tenderloin
    Sea salt
    Freshly ground pepper
    1 tablespoon olive oil
    1 tablespoon butter
    3 ounces fresh *foie gras*
    4 ounces Truffle Sauce (page 234)
    2 slivers of truffle (optional)

## TO PREPARE THE ENDIVE:

Remove any dark outer leaves and cut away the stem of the endives.

Cut the prepared endives into a large julienne.

Place the julienned endives in a bowl and toss with the lemon juice.

Melt the butter in a small sauté pan over medium heat.

When the butter begins to foam, add the endives and wilt for 1-2 minutes, tossing occasionally. Add the paprika, salt, pepper, and the heavy cream.

Bring to a boil and allow the cream to thicken slightly, 1-2 minutes.

Taste and adjust seasonings.

May be prepared ahead and reheated just prior to serving.

## TO PREPARE THE BEEF:

Using a sharp knife dipped in hot water, cut the *foie gras* into 2 medallions. Cut away any blood spots with the tip of the knife blade. Lightly salt and pepper the medallions.

Trim any fat and silver skin from the tenderloin. Cut the tenderloin in half forming 2 medallions. Season the medallions with salt and pepper. Set aside and keep covered.

Heat the truffle sauce, taste, and adjust seasonings. Set aside.

Combine the butter and oil in a heavy skillet over high heat. When the butter begins to brown, sear the medallions of beef. Sauté about 2-3 minutes per side for medium-rare.

Transfer the filets mignons to serving plates and place in a low oven to keep warm.

Wipe out the skillet and return to moderate heat. Add the prepared slices of *foie gras* and sauté them about 10 seconds per side. The *foie gras* should remain pink inside.

## TO SERVE:

Remove the plate from the oven and carefully transfer a slice of *foie gras* on top of each medallion of beef. Garnish the *foie gras* with a slice of truffle, if desired. Pour the truffle sauce around the medallions of beef and serve any remaining sauce on the side.

Serve with the endive gratin.

# Poached Beef Tenderloin

*The tenderloin is the best cut—only the best for your sweetheart. Poached beef tenderloin is one of my personal favorites because it features lightly cooked vegetables and tender beef in a flavor-packed consommé. The reason it is so nourishing and satisfying is the gelatin which aides the digestion.*

THE BEEF:

> 3 quarts Beef Consommé (page 240)
> 2 whites of leek
> 2 stalks of celery
> 2 carrots
> 1 medium turnip
> 1 medium potato
> 12-14 ounces beef tenderloin, filet mignon

THE SAUCE:

> $\frac{1}{4}$ cup Consommé
> 3 tablespoons heavy whipping cream
> 2 teaspoons chopped fresh tarragon
> 1 tablespoon butter

## TO PREPARE THE VEGETABLES:

Trim and clean the leeks and celery stalks. Peel the carrots, turnip, and potato. Cut and portion the vegetables to obtain four 2-inch pieces of each. Poach each separately in 1 cup of the consommé.

Approximate cooking times: leeks, celery and turnips - 5 minutes.
> potatoes - 8 minutes
> carrots - 10 minutes

Reserve each prepared vegetable covered in the Consommé.

## TO PREPARE THE BEEF:

Trim any fat or silver skin from the tenderloin. Tie the beef tenderloin around the center with a length of kitchen twine, leaving approximately a 1 foot length attached.

186

Bring 2 quarts of the Consommé to a boil in a tall medium saucepan. Lower the beef into the boiling broth and secure the twine to the saucepan handle or to a kitchen spoon placed across the top of the saucepan, suspending the beef in the Consommé away from the bottom and sides.

Reduce heat and simmer the beef for 10 minutes for medium rare.

## TO PREPARE THE SAUCE:

While the meat is cooking, bring $1/2$ cup of the Consommé, 3 tablespoons of heavy whipping cream, and 2 teaspoons of finely chopped tarragon to a boil. Boil for 5 minutes to thicken sauce. Remove from heat and whisk in 1 tablespoon of butter. Taste and adjust seasonings.

## TO SERVE:

Heat the prepared vegetables in the Consommé in which they were cooked.

When the meat is cooked to desired doneness, remove from the Consommé. Cut away the twine and cut the filet mignon into 4 filets. Place the 2 sections in the center of each warm plate, with the inside cuts facing up to show doneness.

Arrange the vegetables and pour the sauce around the beef.

Garnish with sprigs of whole tarragon and a pinch of coarse sea salt on the meat.

*Variation:* A tomato sauce is often served with the poached beef. A few tablespoons of the Consommé may also be substituted for a sauce and is actually my personal favorite.

*Hint:* For a better tasting Consommé and food in general use pure water. At home I use a reverse osmosis filter.

# Beef Wellington with Roasted Shiitake Mushrooms

*The classic Filet de Boeuf Wellington or Beef Wellington is named after Arthur Wellesley, first duke of Wellington who defeated Napoleon at Waterloo. Shiitake mushrooms are originally from Japan and Korea. This earthy mushroom is now being cultivated in the United States where it is often called "golden oak." The firm flesh has an almost meaty flavor.*

THE BEEF:

> 1 16-18 ounce center cut of beef tenderloin
> Sea salt
> Freshly ground pepper
> 3-4 ounces pâté of *foie gras*
> 1 tablespoon butter
> 1 tablespoon oil
> 10-12 ounces of Puff Pastry (page 248)
> 2 eggs, beaten (egg wash)
> $^1/_4$ cup Truffle Sauce (page 234)

THE MUSHROOMS:

> 6-8 medium shiitake mushrooms
> 2-3 tablespoons olive oil
> $^1/_2$ teaspoon finely chopped garlic
> Pinch of sea salt
> Pinch freshly ground pepper

## TO PREPARE THE WELLINGTON:

Trim any fat and silver skin that covers the meat.

Using a sharp knife, form a "pocket" in the beef tenderloin by making an incision beginning $^1/_2$-inch back from the tip of the meat. Cut halfway into the meat and stop $^1/_2$-inch before reaching the other end. Lightly salt and pepper the "pocket" and stuff with the *foie gras*, cut lengthwise. Shape the meat and tie with kitchen twine to keep the *foie gras* from falling out.

Season the meat with salt and pepper. Heat the butter and oil in a heavy skillet over high heat. When the butter browns, sear the meat well all around. Place the skillet in a preheated oven for about 10 minutes. Using tongs, turn the meat several times to ensure even cooking.

Remove the meat from the pan and allow to cool completely before wrapping in the puff pastry dough. Remove string when cooled.

Roll the puff pastry dough on a floured surface into a rectangle, approximately 10-inches x 12-inches x $\frac{1}{8}$-inch. Brush off any excess flour.

Place the cooled prepared beef in the center of the puff pastry dough.

Brush the dough with the egg wash and completely envelop the meat. Trim away any excess dough. Chill for at least 1 hour.

*Preheat the oven to 450 degrees.*

Place the uncooked Wellington on an ungreased sheet pan. Brush the surface with the egg wash. Bake for approximately 20 minutes for medium rare. Remove from oven and allow to rest in a warm place for 12-15 minutes before serving. Use a meat thermometer to test for doneness.

While the Wellington is baking, prepare the mushrooms.

## TO PREPARE THE MUSHROOMS:

*Preheat oven to 450 degrees*

Detach the stems from the mushrooms and reserve stems for use in a stock. Wash the mushrooms in cold water twice, lifting them from the water so that the grit stays in the bottom of the bowl.

Thoroughly pat the mushrooms dry. Lightly salt and pepper the mushrooms.

Place the olive oil and garlic in a small bowl. Dip each mushroom in the oil to coat lightly, allowing oil to drain off the mushrooms.

Place the mushrooms on a small baking sheet and place in the preheated oven for 8 minutes.

Remove the mushrooms from the oven and set aside.

*Hint:* Mushrooms may be prepared ahead and reheated in a 400 degree oven for 3-4 minutes.

## TO SERVE:

Cut the Wellington into $\frac{1}{2}$-inch slices and place on a warm serving platter. Serve with the truffle sauce and the roasted shiitake mushrooms.

# Molten Chocolate Cake

*The Aztecs believed in the potency of chocolate, celebrating the cacoa harvest with orgies. The Aztec ruler Montezuma had a harem of several hundred and reportedly drank 50 cups of chocolate daily. Cacao beans were also used as a medium of exchange in the Mayan civilization.*

### THE CHOCOLATE CREAM:

> 2¹/₂ ounces semi-sweet chocolate
> ¹/₂ cup heavy whipping cream
> 2 teaspoons orange liqueur (optional)

### THE CAKE:

> 3 ounces semi-sweet chocolate
> 1¹/₂ tablespoons butter
> 7 teaspoons almond flour
> 4 teaspoons cream of rice
> 3 large eggs
> 4 teaspoons evaporated cane juice or sugar
> 2 ring molds, 3 inches in diameter and 1¹/₂ inches high
> 2 3-inch x 10-inch parchment paper collars
> Butter

## TO PREPARE THE CHOCOLATE CREAM:

Pour the cream in a small heavy-bottomed saucepan and bring to a boil over high heat. Reduce heat and add the 2¹/₂ ounces of chocolate broken into small pieces. Stir constantly with a spoon until the chocolate is completely melted. Remove from heat and stir in the orange liqueur. Transfer to a bowl and refrigerate for at least 2 hours until the mixture is firm.

## TO PREPARE THE CAKE:

Separate the eggs, making certain that the whites are free of any yolk. Whip the yolks and 2 teaspoons of evaporated cane juice in a small glass or stainless steel bowl until the mixture whitens and forms a ribbon, about 1 minute. Fold in the remaining ingredients with a rubber spatula. Set aside.

Whip the egg whites with a pinch of salt in a separate bowl. Beat at low speed; then gradually increase speed while adding the remaining evaporated cane juice. Stop whipping when the whites form soft peaks. Be careful not to over whip.

Gently fold the whites into the yolk mixture with a rubber spatula. Pipe the mixture halfway up into the prepared ring molds. With a medium ice cream scoop, form 2 balls of the thickened chocolate cream and place one in each half-filled cylinder. Pipe the remaining mixture into the prepared ring molds, filling them up. Freeze a minimum of 6 hours. (Best done the day before and frozen overnight.)

*TO SERVE:*

*Preheat oven to 400 degrees.*

Place the frozen cakes in a small baking pan.

Bake in the preheated oven for 20 minutes.

Remove from the oven and allow to rest for 5 minutes.

With the aid of a spatula, transfer each cake to a serving plate.

Carefully run the blade of a small paring knife around the inside of the metal mold. Carefully lift off the mold with the parchment paper collar. Garnish with crème fraîche or ice cream and serve immediately.

# Raspberry Soufflés

*Your guest must be waiting for the soufflé to arrive, as it must be taken directly from oven to table. Raspberries are the most perfumed of the berries, exotic with a slightly musky aroma.*

THE MOLDS:

> 2 1-cup ramekins
> 2 tablespoons unsalted butter
> 1/2 cup granulated evaporated cane juice or sugar

THE SOUFFLÉS:

> 1 cup basic Pastry Cream (page 255)
> 2/3 cup Raspberry Sauce (page 253)
> 2 egg yolks
> 2-3 tablespoons raspberry brandy
> 6 egg whites
> Pinch of sea salt
> Confectioners sugar

*Preheat the oven to 400 degrees.*

Butter and sugar the ramekins.

Place the pastry cream in a large bowl and thoroughly whisk in the egg yolks, 1/3 cup raspberry sauce, and raspberry brandy, if desired.

Place the egg whites and pinch of salt in a mixing bowl. Whip until soft peaks form. Fold the egg whites into the prepared pastry cream. Fill the prepared soufflé molds to the rim, being careful that none of the mixture spills over the sides of the ramekins. Set the molds on the center shelf of the oven and bake for approximately 25 minutes, until the soufflés are well risen.

When the soufflés are ready, remove from the oven, dust with powdered sugar, and serve at once. After presenting at table, break open the top of each with a spoon and pour in a little of the remaining raspberry sauce.

# Crêpes Suzettes

*Perfect for a heated finale, flaming desserts like Crêpes Suzette are pleasing to the eyes as well as the tongue. We do not know the original Suzette, a nickname for Suzanne, this exciting sweet was named for. Chefs often name dishes after their paramours, so I suspect there may have also been Crêpes Jacqueline, Carol, Brigitte, etc.*

> 2-3 oranges
> 1 teaspoon finely grated orange rind
> 3 tablespoons evaporated cane juice or sugar
> 2 tablespoons Grand Marnier or orange liqueur
> 2 tablespoons butter
> 4 Crêpes (page 251)

Grate one of the oranges to obtain 1 teaspoon of rind.

Press the oranges to obtain 1 cup of juice.

Place the orange juice, orange rind, 2 tablespoons evaporated cane juice, and butter in a large shallow saucepan. Over high heat, bring the liquid to a boil and allow to reduce and thicken to the consistency of a light syrup for approximately 2 minutes. Reduce heat.

Place crêpes, one at a time, into the warm liquid and turn to coat both sides. Fold each in half and then into quarters, and place the folded crêpes on one side of the pan until all have been soaked and folded. Raise heat. Move crêpes to the center of the pan and sprinkle with remaining cane juice, douse with the Grand Marnier and ignite. Move pan back and forth to completely flame the Grand Marnier. Remove from heat.

## TO SERVE:

Divide the crêpes and sauce between two warm serving plates and serve at once.

*Variation:* Garnish the plates with orange sections.

# Truffle Ice Cream

*You might be shocked at this combination, but the element of surprise certainly adds to a lusty meal. Actually the rich earthy truffle gives a very exotic undertone to the velvety ice cream.*

For 1 quart:

> 2 ounces truffles
> 1 1/2 cups milk
> 5 large egg yolks
> 2/3 cup evaporated cane juice or honey
> 1 1/2 cups heavy whipping cream

Place over high heat and scald the milk, heating until milk just begins to boil. Remove from heat and allow the truffles to steep in the milk for 15 minutes.

While the truffles are steeping, place the honey in a bowl and place over a pot of boiling water to slightly soften to pouring consistency. Honey should be barely warm to the touch. Try to use a neutral flavored honey.

Beat the egg yolks with a wire whisk in a medium mixing bowl and add the softened honey, mixing thoroughly.

Remove the truffles from the scalded milk. Slowly pour the warm milk into the yolk and honey mixture, whisking constantly. Transfer the mixture back to the saucepan. Cook over simmering water or low direct heat until the custard just barely begins to boil. Remove from heat and immediately pour in the heavy cream. Cool and refrigerate.

Peel the truffles. Coarsely chop 1/2 of the truffles and all the peelings and mix into the prepared custard.

Freeze the custard according to the directions for your machine. The ice cream is ready when it loses its sheen. Place in a covered freezer container and harden before serving.

Slice the remaining truffle into a julienne and sprinkle over the ice cream before serving.

*Hint:* The night before making the ice cream, place whole eggs and truffles in a bowl. Cover tightly with plastic wrap and set in refrigerator overnight. The eggs will absorb the truffle fragrance.

# Individual Baked Alaska

*This dish was supposedly created in New York at Delmonicos Restaurant in honor of the newly purchased territory of Alaska. This is called* Omelette Norvégienne *in France. The novelty of this dessert lies in the contrast between the frozen ice cream inside and the very hot surrounding meringue.*

THE BASE:

> 2 4-inch x $\frac{1}{2}$-inch diameter circles of chocolate sponge cake,
>     (page 250), $\frac{1}{2}$ ounce each
> 2 tablespoons Pastry Syrup (page 252)
> 2 tablespoons orange liqueur or brandy to complement ice cream
> 2 large scoops of ice cream, your choice of flavors

THE MERINGUE:

> 1 cup evaporated cane juice or sugar
> $\frac{1}{2}$ cup water
> 4 large egg whites
> Pinch of sea salt
> $\frac{1}{2}$ teaspoon grated lemon rind
> $\frac{1}{2}$ teaspoon grated orange rind
> $\frac{1}{2}$ teaspoon vanilla extract

Bake a sheet of sponge cake about $\frac{1}{2}$-inch thick. Using a 4-inch cookie cutter, cut 2 circles out of the cake and place them on a small baking sheet.

Mix 1 tablespoon of the liqueur with the syrup and imbibe the cake circles with the mixture, using a small pastry brush.

Place 1 large or 2 small scoops of ice cream in the center of the cake circles. Two small scoops of different flavored ice cream may be stacked. Place in freezer while preparing the meringue.

## TO PREPARE THE MERINGUE:

Prepare an Italian meringue by combining the water and evaporated cane juice or sugar in a small heavy saucepan and boiling until the mixture reaches 280 degrees on a candy thermometer. When the temperature reaches 250 degrees, begin whipping the egg whites and pinch of salt in an electric mixer. Whip until soft peaks form. Stop whipping and wait for the temperature to reach 280 degrees. Remove the saucepan from heat and with the mixer on low, slowly pour the boiled sugar into the egg whites. Add the lemon rind, orange rind, and vanilla extract and continue whipping for about 4 minutes to cool the meringue.

## TO ASSEMBLE THE BAKED ALASKA:

*Preheat the oven to 450 degrees.*

Remove the prepared cake circles with ice cream from the freezer and place on a sheet pan.

Place the cooled meringue in a pastry bag fitted with a star tube.

Beginning on the circle of sponge cake, cover the ice cream completely by forming ascending concentric circles of meringue.

Use any extra meringue to further decorate the 2 Baked Alaskas.

Place the sheet pan in the preheated oven and bake until nicely browned, about 5-6 minutes.

Remove from the oven and place each Baked Alaska on a warm plate. Pour 2 teaspoons of slightly heated brandy over each dessert and flame in front of your guest.

*Variation:* Substitute 2 large cookies for the cake circles.

# Champagne Mousse

*Described as "like the laugh of a pretty girl," champagne is the perfect libation for any romantic repast.*

2 egg yolks
3 tablespoons evaporated cane juice or sugar
²/₃ cup champagne
¹/₂ teaspoon gelatin
1 tablespoon water
¹/₂ cup heavy whipping cream

Whip the heavy cream and refrigerate.

Combine the yolks and evaporated cane juice in a glass or stainless steel bowl and whisk thoroughly until the mixture whitens. Add the champagne and whisk together completely.

Place the bowl over a pot of simmering water and cook, beating constantly until the mixture thickens to the consistency of a light hollandaise sauce. Remove from heat and continue whisking for about 1 minute. Set aside and allow to cool.

Combine the gelatin and water in a small bowl and let stand for 5 minutes to soften the gelatin. Heat the softened gelatin mixture until the gelatin dissolves and the liquid clears.

Whisk the dissolved gelatin into the champagne mixture. Then fold in the whipped cream with the aid of a rubber spatula. Chill for 1 hour before piping the mousse into champagne glasses.

Garnish with fruit marinated in champagne.

# Hazelnut Soufflés

*Evaporated cane juice is dehydrated whole sugar cane sap. A healthier alternative to white sugar, it is rich in chromium, magnesium, silica, and other minerals. Use it one for one in place of white sugar.*

THE SAUCE:

> ¹/₃ cup Vanilla Custard Sauce (page 252)
> 2 teaspoons Hazelnut Paste (page 254)
> 1 tablespoon hazelnut liqueur or Cognac, if desired

THE RAMEKINS:

> 2 1-cup ramekins
> 2 tablespoons unsalted butter
> ¹/₂ cup evaporated cane juice or sugar

THE SOUFFLÉS:

> 1 cup basic Pastry Cream (page 255)
> ¹/₂ cup Hazelnut Paste (page 254)
> 2 egg yolks
> 2 tablespoons Frangelico (hazelnut liqueur), if desired
> 6 egg whites
> Pinch of sea salt
> Confectioners sugar (optional)

## TO PREPARE THE SAUCE:

Combine all of the ingredients in a mixing bowl and whisk thoroughly. Taste and add more liqueur, if desired.

## TO PREPARE THE RAMEKINS:

Generously butter the ramekins with particular attention to the rims. Sugar the ramekins.

## TO PREPARE THE SOUFFLÉS:

*Preheat the oven to 400 degrees.*

Place the pastry cream in a large bowl and thoroughly whisk in the egg yolks, ¹/₂ cup hazelnut butter, and hazelnut liqueur, if desired.

Place the egg whites and pinch of salt in a mixing bowl. Whip until soft peaks form. Fold the egg whites into the prepared pastry cream. Fill the prepared soufflé ramekins to the rim, being careful that none of the mixture spills over the sides of the ramekins. Set the ramekins on the center shelf of the oven and bake for approximately 25 minutes, until the soufflés are well risen and browned on top.

## TO SERVE:

When the soufflés are ready, remove from the oven, dust with powdered sugar, and serve at once. After presenting at table, break open the top of each with a spoon and pour in a little of the prepared sauce. Serve the remaining sauce on the side.

# After Midnight

You have just returned from the theater or an evening of dancing. A little something is needed before bedtime. One dish, perhaps, served in front of the fire or by candlelight might just be perfect to make the end of the evening even more romantic.

These dishes are simple to make and assemble when you return from a night out or they can be completely prepared ahead and served as desired.

The right finishing touch can make the night last forever.

# Suggested Menus

♦♦♦

Oysters with Mignonnette Sauce
Pears Poached in Red Wine


Tartare of Arctic Char
Frozen Honey Soufflés


Sea Bass with Caviar
Champagne Sorbet


Steak Tartare
Hot Spiced Wine


Wild Duck Breast and Foie Gras Salad
Izarra Mousse

# Blinis with Beluga Caviar

*Caviar is considered one of the great love foods. This delicacy will be most appreciated by your special someone. Beluga, with the largest eggs that are dark steel-gray in color, is the most expensive caviar. Made from buckwheat, Russian blinis are traditionally served with caviar and sour cream.*

THE BATTER:

> 1 cup milk
> $^1/_2$ package dry yeast
> $^1/_2$ cup warm water
> 1 cup sifted whole wheat pastry flour
> $^1/_2$ cup sifted buckwheat flour
> 2 medium eggs, separated
> 1 teaspoon evaporated cane juice or sugar
> $^1/_2$ teaspoon sea salt
> 1 $^1/_2$ tablespoons sour cream
> 2 tablespoons butter

THE FINISHING:

> Butter
> Oil
> 2 teaspoons créme fraîche
> 1 ounce Beluga caviar

## TO PREPARE THE BATTER:

Scald $^1/_2$ cup of milk, remove from heat, and allow to cool to lukewarm. Dissolve the yeast in the warm water and add to the cooled milk.

Combine $^1/_2$ of the pastry flour and buckwheat flour and stir into the prepared milk. Cover with a towel and let stand in a warm place for 2$^1/_2$-3 hours. Stir well and fold in the remaining flour and buckwheat flour. Cover and allow to rise for 2 hours.

Scald the remaining milk and allow to cool to lukewarm.

Beat the eggs lightly with a wire whisk. Heat the butter until it just begins to brown and remove from heat.

Whip the egg whites until soft peaks are formed.

Mix the dough with a rubber spatula and fold in the milk, browned butter, eggs, salt, evaporated cane juice, and sour cream. Mix until smooth and then fold in the egg whites. Cover and set aside for $\frac{1}{2}$ hour.

## TO PREPARE THE BLINIS:

Use a heavy iron skillet or griddle to cook the blinis.

Place the pan over high heat and add a small amount of butter and oil, just enough to coat the bottom of the pan. When the butter begins to brown, remove the pan from the heat and ladle about 2 tablespoons of batter into the pan per blini. Each blini should be 2-3 inches in diameter.

Cook until the bottom is nicely brown and bubbles form on the top. Turn with a spatula and fry for another $\frac{1}{2}$ minute or until brown.

Blinis may be prepared ahead and refrigerated before using.

## TO SERVE:

Place a small dollop of crème fraîche or sour cream in the center of each blini, and top each with caviar.

*Hint:* You did not hear this from me but whole buckwheat pancake mixes will do the trick with much less effort. Freeze any remaining blinis for later use.

# Oyster Soup

*The reputation of oysters as an aphrodisiac has been confirmed. They contain zinc and other important trace minerals important for testosterone production.*

10-12 oysters
2 tablespoons butter
2 teaspoons finely chopped shallots
2 tablespoons finely diced celery
2 tablespoons finely sliced Belgian endive
2 cups heavy whipping cream
$1/2$ teaspoon grated horseradish
Sea salt
Freshly ground pepper
$1/2$ teaspoon paprika

Shuck the oysters, reserving as much of the oyster liquor as possible.

Melt the butter in a heavy saucepan and add the prepared vegetables. Gently cook the vegetables over medium heat for about 3 minutes until the celery is *al dente*.

Add the reserved oyster liquor, the heavy cream, sea salt and freshly ground pepper. Bring to a boil over high heat. Reduce heat and allow to boil gently for 2-3 minutes.

Remove from heat, add the grated horseradish, taste and adjust seasonings. Set aside.

While the soup is heating, warm two serving bowls in the oven.

When the soup seasonings have been adjusted, place 5-6 oysters in the warmed bowls and pour the soup over oysters.

Sprinkle paprika over the soup, garnish with celery leaves, and serve at once.

*Hint:* Those wishing their oysters cooked more should add them to the soup just as it boils and allow to heat for 2-3 minutes until the edges of the oysters curl.

# Oysters with Mignonnette Sauce

*Among the many legends surrounding Casanova is the story of him regularly enjoying 50 raw oysters, in the nude, for breakfast.*

>   3-6 fresh oysters per person

THE MIGNONNETTE SAUCE:

>   $^1/_2$ cup red wine vinegar
>   2 teaspoons cracked black peppercorns
>   1 teaspoons finely minced shallots
>   $^1/_2$ teaspoon sea salt (approximately)
>   $^1/_2$ teaspoon finely minced chives

Combine all of the ingredients for the sauce in a small mixing bowl, whisk thoroughly, taste, and adjust seasonings.

Wash the oysters, open, and lift off the shallow shell. Be sure to wipe off the oyster knife after opening each oyster. Leave the oysters attached to the bottom (deeper) shell.

Place the oysters on the half shell on special oyster platters or on a bed of crushed ice to hold them level.

Serve oysters with the mignonnette sauce, rye bread, and butter.

*Variation:* There are any number of oysters available, such as Wellfleet, Salt Aires, Belon, Kumamoto, etc.

# Tartare of Arctic Char

*Char tastes rather like salmon but is a smaller fish making it a better size for two. There are both wild and farmed-raised char. Wild fish are preferable from a nutritional point of view, as, in theory, they are able to obtain their normal diets rather than some sort of feed which might not contain all the nutrients the fish require. Capers are the bud of a flowering shrub, which is native to eastern Asia but widespread in the Mediterranean region. Capers are used as a condiment, either pickled in vinegar or preserved in brine.*

6 ounces Arctic char fillet
1 teaspoon extra virgin olive oil
$\frac{1}{2}$ teaspoon finely grated lime zest
$\frac{1}{2}$ teaspoon lime juice
$\frac{1}{2}$ teaspoon finely minced chives
$\frac{1}{3}$ teaspoon sea salt
Freshly ground pepper
Pinch of cayenne pepper
2 Martini glasses
2 radicchio leaves
1 cup mesclun salad
Chive straws
2 thin lime wedges
10 capers
1 teaspoon caviar

Skin the Arctic char and remove any dark blood line down the center of the fillet. Remove any pin bones. Coarsely dice the Arctic char using a very sharp, clean knife, and cutting board. Place in a mixing bowl and refrigerate.

Peel off 2-3 strips of the outer rind of the lime using a potato peeler and finely chop to obtain $\frac{1}{2}$ teaspoon. Cut 2 thin wedges and press the lime to obtain $\frac{1}{2}$ teaspoon of juice.

Add the lime rind and juice, chopped chives, sea salt, pepper, cayenne, and olive oil to the diced Arctic char. Toss well, taste, adjust seasonings, cover, and refrigerate.

## TO SERVE:

Place a radicchio leaf and a small bunch of salad in the bottom and up 1 side of each martini glass. Divide the seasoned tartare between the two glasses over the radicchio leaves. Garnish each tartare with 4-5 capers, a chive straw, and $1/2$ teaspoon caviar. Attach a lime section to the rim of each of the glasses. Serve with toasted slices of country bread.

*Variation:* For a spicy tartare, add $1/2$ teaspoon finely chopped Jalapeño pepper and omit the caviar. Substitute salmon for the Arctic char.

# Wild Mushroom Flan

*Wild mushrooms—chanterelles, morels, girolles, crèpes, hedgehog, chicken of the woods, cauliflower, etc.—are plentiful. Mix several varieties for a truly memorable dish. Sauté the mushrooms over very high heat. If necessary, prepare the mushrooms in two batches as they will boil rather than sauté if overcrowded in the pan.*

THE MUSHROOMS:

> 7 ounces assorted wild mushrooms
> 1 teaspoon butter
> 1/2 teaspoon finely chopped shallots
> Pinch of chopped garlic
> Sea salt
> Freshly ground pepper

THE SAUCE:

> 1/3 cup Aromatic Broth (page 237) or White Stock (page 228)

THE CUSTARD:

> 1 whole egg
> 1/3 cup heavy whipping cream
> Pinch of nutmeg
> Sea salt
> Freshly ground pepper
> 2 4-ounce ramekins
> Butter

## TO PREPARE THE MUSHROOMS:

Trim and thoroughly wash the mushrooms.

Heat the butter in a medium sauté pan. When the butter just begins to brown, add the prepared mushrooms, and sauté for 3-4 minutes, tossing occasionally. Sprinkle with the shallots, garlic, and season with salt and pepper. Toss several times and remove from heat. Transfer the cooked mushrooms to a strainer set over a bowl. Drain well and reserve the juice.

Pick out 4 large whole mushrooms to be used to garnish the flans. Coarsely chop the remaining mushrooms. Reserve 2 rounded tablespoons of the chopped mushrooms for the sauce.

## TO PREPARE THE CUSTARD:

*Preheat the oven to 450 degrees.*

Thoroughly whisk the egg in a bowl and add the remaining ingredients. Blend completely. Taste and adjust seasonings.

Butter the two 4-ounce ramekins. Fill the buttered ramekins, but do not pack, with the mushrooms. Keep any extra chopped mushrooms for the sauce. Fill the ramekins with the custard. Place the 2 prepared ramekins into a small pan or ovenproof dish. Fill halfway with hot tap water. Place the pan on the stove and bring the water to a boil. Transfer the pan to a preheated oven and bake for about 10 minutes, until the custards are set. Test for doneness by inserting a toothpick. If it comes out clean the flans are set.

## TO PREPARE THE SAUCE:

Combine the Vegetable or Chicken Stock and the reserved chopped mushrooms in a small pan and bring to boil. Season with salt and pepper. Remove from heat and transfer contents to a food processor. Process for 1 minute to purée. Taste and adjust seasonings. Set aside.

## TO SERVE THE FLANS:

Heat the flans by simmering in a water bath for about 4 minutes. While the flans are warming, bring the sauce to a boil. Place the garnish mushrooms on the serving plates and warm them in a low oven.

Lift the ramekins out of the water bath and run a knife along the inside. Invert the ramekins onto a serving plate, spoon the sauce around the flans, and garnish with the reserved mushrooms. Serve immediately.

*Hint:* Flans may be prepared up to a day ahead and reheated before serving.

# Nantucket Bay Scallops with Garlic and Herb Butter

*Pernod is a fennel-flavored aperitif popular along the Riviera. Many famous artists have stated that it is a formidable stimulant of the libido.*

> 6 ounces Nantucket Bay scallops (about 20 pieces)
> Sea salt
> Freshly ground pepper
> 2 tablespoons Garlic and Herb Butter (page 32)
> 1 teaspoon Pernod

Rinse the scallops under cold water to remove any grit and drain well.

Place the garlic butter in a medium sauté pan and place over high heat. When the butter melts and just begins to bubble, add the drained scallops. Simmer in the butter for 3-4 minutes until the scallops are just cooked through, tossing occasionally.

Pour the Pernod around the scallops and tilt the pan towards the flame to *flambé.* Toss once and remove from heat.

Divide the scallops and butter between two warm serving dishes. Serve immediately.

*Hint:* These sweet scallops are a delicacy. Pay careful attention as it is very easy to overcook the scallops. I, personally, prefer them slightly under-done. Ignite Pernod with a match if cooking on an electric stove.

# Sea Bass with Caviar

*Sevruga caviar is the smallest and most reasonably priced of the triumvirate of Russian caviars from the Caspian Sea. This genre is known for its small, crisp eggs that are dark gray to black in color.*

THE HERB VINAIGRETTE:

    1 small egg yolk
    1/2 teaspoon Dijon-style mustard
    1/2 teaspoon sea salt
    Freshly ground pepper
    Pinch of cayenne pepper
    1 1/2 tablespoons champagne vinegar
    1/2 teaspoon finely minced shallots
    1/2 teaspoon chopped chives
    1/2 teaspoon finely chopped capers
    1/2 cup olive oil

SPECIAL EQUIPMENT:

    2 ring molds, 3 inches in diameter and 1 1/2 inches high

THE SEA BASS:

    6 ounces of sushi-grade sea bass fillet
    1 teaspoon extra virgin olive oil
    1/2 teaspoon lemon juice
    1/2 teaspoon sea salt
    Freshly ground pepper
    1 ounce caviar

## TO PREPARE THE VINAIGRETTE:

Place the egg yolk and mustard in a small mixing bowl and whisk thoroughly. Add the remaining ingredients, except the oil, and whisk completely. While whisking continuously, slowly pour in the olive oil.

Taste and adjust seasonings. Refrigerate. The vinaigrette may be prepared several hours ahead.

## TO PREPARE THE SEA BASS:

Skin the fillet and cut in half lengthwise. Trim away any skin or blood line that remains on the sea bass. Rinse under cool running water and dry with paper towels. Chill thoroughly by placing in the freezer for 10-12 minutes.

Chop the bass fillet into a small dice and transfer to a small mixing bowl. Cover and refrigerate up to 3 hours if not serving immediately.

## TO SERVE:

Just before serving, season the prepared sea bass with the salt, pepper, lemon juice, and olive oil, tossing with a fork. Add $\frac{1}{2}$ of the caviar and gently mix. Taste and adjust seasonings.

Place a mold in the center of each serving plate. Divide the tartare between the two molds. Press gently to level and shape the tartare. Lift off the mold and top with the remaining caviar. Stir the vinaigrette and spoon around the tartare. Serve any remaining vinaigrette on the side.

Garnish with caper berries.

*Variation:* Substitute black bass or rockfish. Red wine, sherry wine vinegar, or a combination of the two may be used in the vinaigrette.

# Snails and Asparagus in Beer Sabayon

*This is a "wicked" combination, one that is sure to please. I recommend a fairly light beer to avoid a bitter tasting sauce.*

    12 medium asparagus
    20 fresh large snail meats
    1 cup of beer
    2 egg yolks
    1 tablespoon butter
    2 tablespoons heavy whipping cream

Cut the asparagus to obtain 4-inch tips. Wash the asparagus.

Bring the beer to a boil and drop in the asparagus. Reduce heat and simmer until the asparagus are *al dente*, about 2 minutes. Remove the asparagus from the beer with a slotted spoon. Set aside.

Return the pan of beer to flame and bring to a boil. Add snails, reduce heat, and cover. Simmer until tender, approximately 15 minutes. Remove from heat and lift the snails out of the beer with a slotted spoon. Set aside with the prepared asparagus.

Place the pan of beer over high heat, bring to a boil, and reduce volume by two-thirds.

## TO PREPARE THE SAUCE:

While the beer is evaporating, lightly season egg yolks with sea salt and freshly ground pepper and whisk thoroughly in a small bowl. Pour the egg yolks into a stainless steel or glass double boiler. Transfer the reduced beer to the double boiler and whisk thoroughly.

Cook the egg/beer mixture in the double boiler, whisking constantly for 2-3 minutes until the mixture thickens to the consistency of a light hollandaise sauce.

To test for doneness, pull the whisk up out of the sauce; a ribbon, rather than individual, streams should form. Immediately add the butter, whisking continuously until the butter is incorporated into the sauce. Finally whisk in the cream. Taste and adjust seasonings.

*Preheat the broiler.*

Divide the drained asparagus and snails between two gratin dishes. Coat with the sauce and brown lightly under the broiler. Serve immediately.

214

# Mussels Marinières

*This traditional treatment is simple to prepare. The broth is as delicious for sipping as the mussels for eating. Be sure to serve with crusty bread for dipping.*

> 1 pound mussels
> 1 1/2 tablespoons finely chopped shallots
> 1/2 cup dry white wine
> 3 tablespoons butter
> 1 tablespoon finely chopped parsley
> 2 sprigs of fresh thyme
> Sea salt
> Freshly ground pepper

Clean the mussels individually under cold running water, scraping off any clinging barnacles or "beards." Discard any half-open shells or any unusually heavy ones, indicating internal grit. Wash in several changes of cold water, lifting out of the cold water so the sand stays in the bowl.

Place the shallots, white wine, 1 tablespoon of butter, 1/2 tablespoon chopped parsley, sprigs of thyme, pinch of salt, and about 3 turns of the peppermill in a medium saucepan. Bring to a boil over high heat. Reduce and simmer for 3-4 minutes.

Add the mussels and turn up the flame to high. Bring to a boil, cover, and allow to cook for about 4 minutes or until all the mussels are open. Shake the pan of mussels once or twice while cooking.

Remove mussels from the saucepan with the aid of a slotted spoon. Return pan to high heat and reduce the broth by a third, about 2-3 minutes.

While the broth is boiling, pull the top shell off of each mussel and divide the prepared mussels between two warm bowls.

Cover, if holding for a few minutes, and keep warm in a low oven.

After reducing the broth, whisk in the remaining butter and chopped parsley. Taste and adjust seasonings and pour over the mussels. Serve.

*Hint:* Buy so called "rope" mussels. They are suspended off the bottom in sacks and for the most part are much cleaner outside with less internal grit. May be prepared ahead. To reheat, boil the broth, add the mussels, and steam for 1 minute.

# Salmon with Port Wine Sauce

*This warm and cozy dish will be happily received by your guest at any time of the year. A totally simple yet satisfying dish.*

> 8 ounces salmon fillet, approximately $1/2$-inch thick
> 2 tablespoons butter
> 1 tablespoon olive oil
> $1/3$ cup port wine
> $1/2$ cup heavy whipping cream
> 2 teaspoons tomato purée
> Sea salt
> Freshly ground pepper

Cut the skinned salmon fillet into 2 portions. Lightly salt and pepper.

In a medium sauté pan, combine the butter and oil. Place over medium heat. When the butter just begins to brown, add the salmon fillets. Cook approximately 2 minutes on one side, turn the fillets, cover the pan, and cook another 5 minutes or until just cooked through. Transfer the salmon to two serving plates and keep warm.

Pour the fat out of the sauté pan and place over high heat. Deglaze the pan with the port wine and add the heavy cream and tomato purée. Bring to a boil and reduce the liquid by half. Taste and adjust seasonings.

Coat the salmon fillets with the warm sauce and serve at once.

Serve with Brown Rice Pilaf (page 51).

# Steak Tartare

*The name comes from the fierce Tartars who assembled a large empire while eating raw meat. This is my favorite luncheon dish when I am in Paris. Eat raw beef and you just might conquer the world.*

8-10 ounces beef tenderloin tips or flank steak
2 tablespoons finely minced onion
1 tablespoon finely chopped parsley
1 teaspoon finely chopped capers
1 teaspoon Dijon-style mustard
1 teaspoon salad or olive oil
Pinch of cayenne pepper
Few drops Cognac
$\frac{1}{2}$ teaspoon of Worcestershire sauce
Few drops of red wine vinegar
Sea salt
Freshly ground pepper
2 egg yolks
1 hard boiled egg, yolk and white chopped separately

## TO PREPARE:

Trim the fat and any silver skin from the beef.

Cut the beef into a julienne and coarsely chop.

Place the chopped beef in a medium bowl. Add the onion, parsley, capers, mustard, oil, and seasonings. Mix thoroughly with a spoon or rubber spatula. Taste and adjust seasonings.

Form the prepared beef into 2 patties. Place each on a separate plate. Using the back of a teaspoon, form a depression in the center of each patty. Place an egg yolk in the depression.

Garnish the plate with the chopped hard boiled egg and serve with toasted slices of country bread.

*Hint:* $\frac{1}{2}$ teaspoon chopped anchovies makes for a zesty steak tartare. Garnish the plate with additional chopped onions, parsley, and capers. Substitute quail egg yolks.

# Wild Duck Breast
# and Foie Gras Salad

*Casanova recommended foie gras as one of the best delicacies to serve your intended. This combination is both seductive and unusual.*

1 wild duck: Mallard, Pintail, Black Duck
3 ounces duck *foie gras*
1 tablespoon butter
1 teaspoon extra virgin olive oil
Sea salt
Freshly ground pepper
2 quail eggs
2 ounces mesclun salad (about 2 cups)
1/2 cup Vinaigrette (page 245)
6 cherry tomatoes
8 cucumber slices

## TO PREPARE THE DUCK:

Debone the duck by placing it breast up with the cavity facing you. Grasp the left thigh, pull it away from the carcass, and then cut down through the joint to separate it. Turn the duck so the neck faces you and remove the other thigh. Remove the breast by running the knife along one side of the breastbone and scraping the meat off along the rib cage. Cut through and detach the wing joint at the shoulder. Repeat on the other side. Finally, cut away the wing joint attached to each breast, leaving 2 duck "steaks." Lightly salt and pepper and reserve.

The legs are tough and are usually stewed.

## TO PREPARE THE FOIE GRAS:

Using a sharp knife dipped in hot water, cut the *foie gras* into 2 equal portions. Lightly salt and pepper and dust with flour, brushing off any excess. Reserve.

## TO PREPARE THE QUAIL EGGS:

Carefully crack the eggs to keep the yolks intact, into two small dishes or cups and reserve.

*TO PREPARE THE GREENS:*

Wash and thoroughly drain the greens and reserve in a mixing bowl.

*TO PREPARE THE SALAD:*

In a medium sauté pan, heat 2 tablespoons of butter and 1 tablespoon of oil. When the butter begins to brown, add the breasts, skin side down. Sauté for about 1½ minutes. Then, turn the breasts and cook an additional 1½ minutes for medium rare, depending on the thickness of the duck breasts. Increase the cooking time to suit individual taste. Remove from the pan and set aside.

Immediately drain the fat from the pan and return to medium heat. Add 1 tablespoon of butter. When the butter just begins to brown, carefully pour in the quail eggs and cook to taste; I prefer just set. Transfer the fried quail eggs to a plate with a spatula.

Immediately add the slices of *foie gras* and sauté them for about 10 seconds per side. Do not overcook—the liver should be pink inside. Transfer the *foie gras* slices to the same plate as the quail eggs.

*TO COMPOSE THE SALAD:*

Add the Vinaigrette to the prepared greens and toss.

Divide the greens, cherry tomatoes, and cucumber slices between two serving plates.

Cut the cooked duck breasts into thin diagonal slices and arrange slices on the plates next to the greens. Place a slice of *foie gras* on the greens and a quail egg on the *foie gras*. Serve immediately.

*Variation:* Use Mallard duck breasts instead of the wild duck.

*Hint:* I use the duck bones and legs to make a duck stock or soup.

# Champagne Sorbet

*This ultimate sorbet is a distinctly refreshing dessert. It is also perfect for cleansing the palate between the courses of a romantic repast.*

> $^1/_2$ cup water
> $^2/_3$ teaspoon gelatin
> 1 teaspoons lemon zest
> 1 cup evaporated cane juice or sugar
> $^1/_2$ bottle of champagne

Combine the water and gelatin. Allow 5 minutes for the gelatin to soften. Add the other ingredients, except the champagne, and bring to a boil. Remove from heat and allow the mixture to cool and infuse for 1 hour. Add champagne and freeze according to the instructions for your ice cream freezer.

Serve with berries macerated in champagne and garnish with mint leaves.

*Hint:* If you do not have an ice cream freezer, you may use a food processor to make the sorbet. Place all the ingredients in the processor and mix well. Freeze mixture. Remove from freezer and process again. Return to freezer.

Serve the sorbet by scooping into a champagne glass and pouring champagne into the glass. *Voila!*

# Pears Poached in Wine with Cassis Sorbet

*This is a classic dessert that is easy to prepare. Anjou pears are thought to have come from France near the village of Angers and were introduced to America just before the Civil War. Anjou are the principal variety grown in this country. Cassis are black currants. This sorbet may be used to cleanse the palate between courses or to serve with summer berries and fruits.*

## The Sorbet:

Makes 1 pint

> 2 pints black currants
> 1 cup evaporated cane juice

Remove any stems from the berries and purée in a food processor. Strain forcefully through a fine sieve, to obtain 2 cups of seedless purée. Thoroughly whisk the evaporated cane juice into purée.

Freeze according to the directions on your ice cream machine. The sorbet should stiffen in about 20 minutes. Cover and freeze.

## The Fruit:

> 2 ripe pears, Anjou or Bartlett
> $\frac{1}{2}$ cup honey, evaporated cane juice, or sugar
> 2 cups red wine
> 1 clove
> 1 inch piece of cinnamon
> $\frac{1}{4}$ teaspoon each grated lemon and orange rind

Combine the sweetener, red wine, spices, and grated rinds in a small saucepan just large enough to hold the 2 pears and syrup and bring to a boil over high heat. Reduce heat and simmer for 5 minutes to infuse wine with spices.

Peel and core pears just as the syrup is ready. Place them in the syrup and bring to a boil. As soon as the syrup boils, test for doneness by inserting a sharp knife into the pear. Ripe pears might need no further cooking. Keep pears fairly firm.

Remove the saucepan from heat. Set aside and allow the pears to cool in the syrup.

Remove pears from the syrup and set aside. Strain to remove spices. Bring syrup to a boil over high heat and reduce by two-thirds, about 8 minutes, to make a sauce to accompany the pears.

Pour the warm reduced syrup over the pears just before serving.

Serve with Cassis sorbet.

# Chocolate Cream Puffs

*Sweet cream puffs are filled with pastry cream, whipped cream, ice cream, jam, etc. It is not practical to make a smaller amount of the dough.*

Makes about 20 cream puffs.

### THE CREAM PUFF DOUGH:

> 1 cup water
> 1 stick unsalted butter
> $1^3/_4$ tablespoons evaporated cane juice or sugar
> $^1/_4$ teaspoon sea salt
> $^1/_4$ pound sifted flour
> 4 whole medium eggs
> Chocolate ice cream

Place the water, butter, sugar, and salt in a shallow heavy-bottomed saucepan over medium heat. Let the mixture come to a boil, stirring from time to time. Remove from heat and rapidly incorporate the sifted flour using a wooden spoon. Stir vigorously to completely blend all of the ingredients.

Return the saucepan to burner on medium heat. Stir the dough continuously until it dries somewhat and no longer sticks to the sides of the pan or the wooden spoon, about 2 minutes.

Remove from heat and transfer dough to a mixing bowl.

Using an electric mixer or rubber spatula, add the eggs, one at a time. Scrape the sides and bottom of the bowl to thoroughly blend all of the ingredients.

The number and size of the eggs are important when preparing this dough. A dough that is too firm will cause the cream puffs to be underdeveloped and heavy; a soft mixture will produce very light and fragile cream puffs.

Place the prepared dough in a pastry bag with a large plain tube and portion out on a lightly buttered baking pan. Bake immediately in a pre-heated 425 degree oven for approximately 30 minutes.

Allow to cool completely before removing from pan and storing.

### TO SERVE:

Fill with slightly softened chocolate ice cream with the aid of a pastry bag fitted with a star tube. Freeze the cream puffs until just a few minutes before serving. Dust with cocoa powder before presenting.

*Hint:* Freeze remaining cream puffs for later use.

# Izarra Mousse

*Izarra, the liqueur originating in the Basque area of southwest France, was originally an herbal elixir or tonic used for medicinal purposes. The liqueur is either green or yellow. In this recipe, I have used the saffron-based yellow Izarra. Since Izarra is somewhat difficult to find, I suggest Chartreuse or other herbed liqueurs as substitutes.*

> 1 cup of heavy whipping cream
> 2 teaspoons honey
> $1/2$ teaspoon gelatin
> 1 tablespoon water
> $1/2$ cup Izarra

Whip the heavy cream in a medium mixing bowl and chill.

Combine the water and gelatin in a small mixing bowl. Allow 5 minutes for the gelatin to soften. Add the honey and set over a pot of boiling water. Heat for 1-2 minutes until the gelatin melts. Whisk thoroughly. Add the Izarra and mix completely.

Fold the Izarra mixture into the heavy whipping cream with the aid of a rubber spatula.

Pipe or spoon the mousse into $1/2$-cup size or larger stemware or dishes. Top the mousse with a few drops of Izarra, if desired.

*Hint:* The $1/2$ cup of Izarra makes for a rather strong mousse. One might begin with a lesser amount and add more to taste.

Crack the bones and cut the carcasses into 2 or 3 pieces with a meat cleaver and rinse well in cold water. Place bones in a large stockpot, cover with the water, and bring to a full boil. Skim thoroughly. Add the vegetables and herbs. Reduce heat and simmer partly covered for 2 to 3 hours, skimming as necessary.

Pour stock through a fine strainer into a bowl. Chill and reserve.

Remove any congealed fat that accumulates on top of the stock before using.

# Lamb Stock

Makes 1 quart

> 2 pounds lamb bones and scraps
> $^1/_2$ carrot
> $^1/_2$ medium onion
> 2-inch piece of celery
> $2^1/_2$ quarts cold water
> 2 tablespoons tomatopurée
> 3 bay leaves
> 3 cloves
> $^1/_2$ teaspoon thyme
> $^1/_2$ teaspoon tarragon
> $^1/_2$ teaspoon cracked black peppercorns
> 1 clove garlic, peeled and crushed

*Preheat oven to 450 degrees.*

Place the bones and scraps in a roasting pan and brown well for 25 to 30 minutes. Coarsely chop the carrot, onion, and celery. Add these to the bones and cook an additional 15 minutes.

Remove the pan from the oven and transfer the bones and meat to a deep stockpot. Deglaze the roasting pan with 1 cup of the water and scrape any meat particles from the bottom. Cover the bones with the deglazing liquid and the rest of the cold water and bring to a full boil. Skim the broth well and add the remaining ingredients. Lower the heat and simmer 2-3 hours. Strain the stock. There should be about 1 quart.

*Hint:* Freeze small quantities in tightly sealed paper cups for later use.

# Lamb Sauce

Makes 2 to 3 cups

> 1½ tablespoons minced shallots
> 1½ tablespoons dry white wine
> 3 tablespoons red wine vinegar
> 1 quart Lamb Stock
> 3 tablespoons red currant jelly
> ½ teaspoon sea salt
> Pinch of freshly ground pepper

Place the shallots, wine, and vinegar in a heavy 3-quart saucepan. Bring to a full boil over high heat and reduce until nearly dry. Add the lamb stock. Bring to a boil and reduce by one-third. Remove from heat, blend in currant jelly with a whisk, and add salt and pepper. Strain and reserve.

# Basic Deer Sauce

Makes 1 quart

> 4 pounds deer bones and trimmings
> 3 cups chopped onions (no need to peel)
> 1½ cups chopped carrots (no need to pare)
> 2 tablespoons flour
> 1 gallon water (approximately)
> 2 tablespoons tomato purée
> 3 bay leaves
> 5 whole cloves
> Pinch of thyme
> 4 sprigs parsley
> ½ teaspoon cracked black peppercorns
> 2 cloves garlic, peeled and crushed
> 8 juniper berries, crushed

Using a meat cleaver, crack and cut the bones into small pieces. Place in a roasting pan and brown in a preheated 375-degree oven, turning occasionally, for about ½ hour. Add the onions and carrots to the partly browned bones and continue cooking until the vegetables are also well browned, about 15 additional minutes.

Dust the bones with the flour, mix well, and transfer the contents of the pan to a large stockpot. Deglaze the roasting pan with 1 cup of the water, scraping any meat particles from the bottom.

Cover the bones with the deglazing liquid and the water. Add the tomato purée, herbs, garlic, and juniper berries. Bring to a boil, reduce the flame, and simmer, partly covered, for 3-4 hours. Reduce the stock until 1 quart remains, skimming occasionally. Strain through a sieve and reserve, discarding the solids.

*Hint:* Dot the top of the sauce with butter to prevent a skin from forming.

# Duck Stock

Makes 2 cups

> 2 duck carcasses with necks and giblets
> 1 large onion, quartered
> ½ cup carrots, coarsely chopped
> 2-inch piece celery, chopped
> 6 cups water (approximately)
> ½ teaspoon cracked black peppercorns
> 1 clove garlic, crushed
> 1 sprig parsley
> 2 bay leaves
> 4 cloves
> Pinch of thyme

*Preheat oven to 400 degrees.*

Cut the carcasses into 4-5 pieces with a meat cleaver and place in a roasting pan with the necks and giblets. Roast in the oven until the bones begin to brown, approximately 20 minutes. Add the onion, carrots, and celery. Roast for another 15 minutes.

Remove the pan from the oven and pour off any fat. Transfer the duck parts and vegetables to a large stockpot. Deglaze the roasting pan with 1 cup of the water and scrape any meat particles from the bottom. Cover the bones with the deglazing liquid and the rest of the water and bring to a boil over high heat. Skim the stock and add all the other ingredients. Lower the heat and simmer, uncovered, for about 2 hours, reducing the liquid by two-thirds. Skim occasionally to remove surface scum.

Strain and carefully degrease before using.

# Basic Beef or Veal Sauce

Makes 1 quart
> 3 pounds veal or beef bones and meat
> 1 cup coarsely chopped onions
> $1/2$ cup coarsely chopped carrots
> 1 2-inch piece of celery
> 3 tablespoons flour
> 2-$2^1/2$ quarts cold water
> 2 tablespoons tomato purée or 1 fresh tomato, chopped
> 2 bay leaves
> 3 whole cloves
> Pinch of thyme
> 4 parsley sprigs (optional)
> $1/2$ teaspoon cracked black peppercorns
> 2 cloves garlic, crushed
> 1 teaspoon butter

Using a meat cleaver, crack and cut the bones into small pieces. Place in a roasting pan and brown in a preheated 375-degree oven for 30 to 40 minutes, stirring occasionally.

Add the onions, carrots, and celery to the partly browned bones and continue cooking until the vegetables are also well browned, approximately 15 more minutes.

Remove pan from oven and drain the fat. Dust the bones with the flour, return pan to the oven, and cook for 5 more minutes.

Transfer the bones and vegetables to a stockpot. Deglaze the roasting pan with 1 cup of the water, scraping any meat particles from the bottom. Cover bones with deglazing liquid and remaining water. Add tomato or tomato purée, herbs, and garlic.

Bring to a boil, reduce heat, and simmer, uncovered, 2½-3 hours. Skim occasionally.

Strain into a bowl and discard solids; 2½-3 cups of stock should remain. Dot the top of the stock with the butter to prevent a skin from forming.

*Hint:* If a sauce is too thin, the easiest way to thicken it is with cornstarch. Place a small amount in a cup and stir in water, a few drops at a time, until a thick paste (the consistency of kindergarten glue) is formed. Whisk a little into the simmering sauce and boil 2-3 minutes. Add more cornstarch until the desired consistency is reached.

# White Butter Sauce

Makes 1 cup

> ½ pound unsalted butter (2 sticks)
> ½ cup dry white wine
> 2 tablespoons white wine vinegar
> 2 tablespoons finely minced shallots
> 1 teaspoon sea salt
> Pinch of freshly ground pepper

Dice the butter and allow to soften slightly.

Combine the wine, vinegar, and shallots in a small saucepan and boil down, until almost dry. Reduce the heat to the lowest setting. Beat in the butter, several pieces at a time. Whisk constantly until all the butter has been incorporated into the sauce and remove from heat. The sauce should have the consistency and appearance of a light hollandaise.

Taste and adjust seasonings. Transfer to a warm sauce boat and serve.

# Madeira Sauce

Serves 4

    $^1/_2$ cup Madeira wine
    $^1/_2$ tablespoon finely minced shallots
    1 cup Basic Beef Sauce (page 232)
    1 tablespoon butter
    Sea salt
    Freshly ground pepper to taste

In a small saucepan over medium-high heat, reduce the Madeira and shallots by half. Add the Basic Beef Sauce. Bring to a boil and simmer 4-5 minutes. Remove from heat and stir in butter with a whisk. Adjust seasonings. You may add a little more Madeira just before serving, if desired.

*Variation:* substitute Sherry or Port for the Madeira.


# Truffle Sauce

    $^1/_2$ cup Port wine
    $^1/_2$ ounce of truffle
    $^1/_2$ cup Basic Veal or Beef Sauce (page 232)
    2 teaspoons butter
    Sea salt
    Freshly ground pepper

Chop the truffle and place in a small saucepan with the Port wine. Place pan over high heat and bring to a boil. Reduce the Port wine by two-thirds and add the Veal or Beef Stock. Bring to boil, reduce heat, and simmer for 3-4 minutes. Remove from heat and whisk in the butter. Taste and adjust seasoning.

*Hint:* Use any truffle peelings accumulated from other recipes. Substitute *foie gras* cut into a small dice for the butter.

# Fish Stock

Makes 1 quart

> $^1/_2$ cup vegetable oil
> 1 cup onions, peeled and sliced
> $^1/_2$ cup carrots, pared and sliced
> $^1/_2$ cup leeks, washed well and sliced
> $^1/_2$ cup celery, sliced
> 2 pounds fish bones (approximately 5 bass or other non-oily fish)
> 1 cup dry white wine
> 1 quart cold water or enough to completely cover fish bones
> 1 bay leaf
> 8 cracked black peppercorns
> 2 cloves
> 3 sprigs parsley
> 2 sprigs thyme or $^1/_4$ teaspoon dried thyme

Heat the oil in a 3-quart stockpot; add the vegetables, cover, and simmer over low heat for about 5 minutes, stirring occasionally, until onion slices are translucent.

Add the fish bones, wine, cold water, and remaining ingredients. Bring to a boil, reduce heat, and simmer uncovered for 25 minutes. Skim as needed.

Remove from heat and strain.

It is important to simmer the Fish Stock for only 25-30 minutes and to strain it immediately to avoid a strong "fishy" taste.

*Hint:* Freeze extra stock for later use.

# Lobster Sauce

Makes 1 quart

> 1 live lobster weighing 1-1½ pounds
> 2 tablespoons olive oil
> ¼ cup each diced leeks (use all parts), carrots, and onions
> 1 2-inch piece of celery
> 2 tablespoons brandy
> 1 cup white wine
> 1 quart Fish Stock (page 235)
> 2 tablespoons tomato paste
> 2 cloves each: shallots and garlic
> 3 bay leaves
> 5 cloves
> ½ teaspoon cracked black peppercorns
> 1 sprig each fresh or ¼ teaspoon dried thyme and tarragon
> ½ tablespoon salt
> 2 tablespoons butter
> 2 tablespoons flour

Split the lobster's head in half lengthwise by inserting the point of a sharp heavy knife where the tail joins the body and cut down through the head. Detach the tail. Remove the claws and crack them with the blunt side of the knife blade. Discard the stomach sac, found in the head. Reserve the green parts (the liver), called tomalley, in a small bowl.

Heat the olive oil in a heavy saucepan over medium heat. Add the vegetables and brown lightly, stirring often.

Add the lobster pieces and juices and cook until the shell reddens. Add the brandy and ignite. When the flames have subsided, pour in the wine and Fish Stock. Add the tomato paste, shallots, garlic, and seasonings.

Simmer 15 minutes and then remove the lobster tail and claws. Extract the meat and reserve. Return the shells to the pot and boil for another 30 minutes.

Remove from the heat. Grind the broth and shells in a food processor. This should be done in several small batches, so as not to overtax the machine. If a processor is not available, drain the liquid from the pot and crush the shells with a large ladle or wooden mallet to extract all of the lobster essence. Return the broth and crushed shells to the pot and bring to a boil.

Blend the butter, tomalley, and flour together and whisk this paste into the liquid. Boil another 10 minutes, then force through a fine sieve.

*Hint:* Dot the top of the sauce with butter to prevent a skin from forming.

# Aromatic Broth

Makes 2 quarts

> 2 quarts water
> 1 cup onions, cut in slivers
> 1 cup carrots, cut in thin rounds
> $\frac{1}{2}$ cup leeks, washed well and sliced
> $\frac{1}{2}$ cup celery, cut in slivers
> 2 bay leaves
> 3 cloves
> $\frac{1}{2}$ teaspoon cracked black peppercorns
> 2 cups dry white wine
> 2 tablespoons white wine vinegar
> 2 tablespoons sea salt

Place all the ingredients in a 3-quart pot and bring to a boil. Reduce the heat and let simmer for 30 minutes, uncovered. Remove from heat and cool.

Transfer liquid and vegetables into a bowl and store in refrigerator until needed.

*Hint:* May be prepared ahead of time or even frozen. Strain the broth to remove the vegetables just prior to use.

# Pork Stock

Makes 2 cups

> 1 pound pork bones
> ½ cup chopped carrot
> ½ cup chopped onion
> 1 tablespoon chopped celery
> 1½ quarts cold water
> 1 tablespoon tomato purée
> 1 bay leaf
> 1 clove
> Pinch of thyme
> ½ teaspoon cracked black peppercorns
> 1 clove garlic, crushed

*Preheat the oven to 450 degrees.*

Chop the bones into 1-2-inch pieces. Place bones and any trimmings in a medium skillet. Place on the flame and brown well for about 10 minutes, tossing the bones and scraping the bottom of the pan. Add the prepared vegetables and place the pan in the oven. Brown for about another 20 minutes, stirring the bones once or twice.

Remove the pan from the oven and transfer the bones to a pot.

Deglaze the skillet with 1 cup of water and bring to a boil. Scrape the meat particles from the skillet and add to the pot.

Cover the bones with the cold water and add the liquid from the skillet. Bring to a boil over high heat and skim the stock.

Add the remaining ingredients. Lower heat and simmer about 1½ hours. Strain the stock. Approximately 2 cups should remain.

# Pork Sauce

For 1 cup

>   1 tablespoon minced shallots
>   3 tablespoons red wine vinegar
>   2 cups Pork Stock (page 238)
>   1-1 1/2 tablespoons red currant jelly
>   Sea salt
>   Freshly ground pepper

Place the shallots and vinegar in a small saucepan. Bring to a boil over high heat and reduce until nearly dry. Add the Pork Stock. Bring to a boil and reduce by half. Remove from heat and whisk in currant jelly to taste. Season with salt and pepper.

# Chicken Stock

Makes 1 quart

>   1 chicken carcass
>   1 medium onion, quartered
>   1/2 cup carrots, coarsely chopped
>   2-inch piece of celery, chopped
>   6 cups of water
>   1/2 teaspoon cracked black peppercorns
>   1 clove of garlic, crushed
>   1 sprig of parsley
>   1 bay leaf
>   3 cloves
>   Pinch of thyme

*Preheat oven to 400 degrees.*

Chop the carcass into 5-6 pieces with a meat cleaver and place in a small roasting pan. Roast in the oven until the bones begin to brown, approximately 20 minutes. Add the onion, carrots, and celery. Roast for another 15 minutes or until the bones are nicely browned, mixing occasionally.

Remove the pan from the oven and pour off any fat. Transfer the bones and vegetables to a large saucepan. Deglaze the roasting pan with 2 cups of water and scrape any meat particles from the bottom.

Cover the bones with the deglazing liquid and the remaining 4 cups of water and bring to a boil over high heat. Skim the stock and add all of the other ingredients. Lower heat and simmer, uncovered, for about 2 hours, reducing the liquid by two-thirds. Skim occasionally to remove surface scum.

Strain and carefully degrease.

*Note:* It is impractical to make in very small quantities. Freeze remaining stock for another use.


# Consommé

Makes 1 gallon:

> 4-5 pounds beef or veal bones and lean trimmings
> (marrow bones and rib and neck bones preferred)
> 1 1/2 gallons cold water
> 1 cup dry white wine
> 1 medium onion
> 1 celery stalk
> 1 white section of one leek
> 1 large carrot
> Small bunch of parsley stems
> 2 bay leaves
> 3 cloves
> Pinch of thyme
> 1 tablespoon sea salt
> 1 teaspoon cracked peppercorns

## STEP 1:

Crack the bones with the aid of a cleaver. Cut the vegetables into large pieces.

Place bones, water, and vegetables in a large stock pot and bring to a boil over high heat. Skim away fat and scum with a ladle.

Lower heat and simmer uncovered for $1/2$ hour, skimming as needed.

Add the remaining ingredients and simmer another 2-3 hours, skimming if needed.

Strain the broth, taste, and adjust seasonings.

## STEP 2:

Clarifying the consommé

    1 pound lean ground beef
    10 egg whites
    2 tablespoons chopped celery
    2 tablespoons chopped carrot
    1 medium onion
    4 cloves
    1 bay leaf
    Sprig of thyme

Cut the onion in half and press 2 cloves into the top of each. Place each, cut side down, over direct high heat and char, approximately 4-5 minutes.

Mix all of the other ingredients together and place in the bottom of a large pot. Add the beef broth and place over high heat. Add the burned onion to the broth and bring to a boil. When the broth begins to boil, reduce heat and simmer for about 4 hours to clarify and strengthen the consommé. Do not stir the broth while simmering.

Taste consommé and adjust seasonings.

Place a large piece of damp gauze or cloth over a strainer resting over a pot or bowl and slowly pour the consommé through the gauze. Try not to disturb the ground meat and egg mass.

Refrigerate the strained consommé. Scrape any fat from the surface of the congealed consommé before using.

# Hollandaise Sauce

Makes ³/₄ cup

> 1 stick butter
> 2 egg yolks
> 1 tablespoon warm water
> Sea salt
> Freshly ground pepper
> Dash of cayenne pepper
> ¹/₂ teaspoon lemon juice

Melt the butter over low heat. Clarify by skimming off the foam and careful-ly pouring off the butter, leaving the milky residue in the bottom of the pan.

In a small stainless steel or glass bowl, whip together the egg yolks and tablespoon of warm water with a whisk until smooth. Avoid aluminum as it discolors the yolks.

Place the bowl over a pan of simmering water to form a double boiler. Beat continuously, using the whisk to scrape the mixture from the bottom and sides of the bowl. Beating vigorously in a figure-8 pattern incorporates more air, and thereby results in a lighter sauce.

To test for doneness, pull the whisk out of the sauce; a thick ribbon rather than individual streams should form.

Remove from heat and slowly add the warm clarified butter, beating con-tinuously. Should the sauce begin to separate, add 1 teaspoon cold water.

Season with lemon juice, salt, and cayenne pepper to taste.

Strain the sauce through a fine sieve into a warm—not hot—stainless steel or nonmetallic bowl.

# Béarnaise Sauce

Makes ³/₄ cup

> ¹/₈ teaspoon cracked black peppercorns
> 1 teaspoon shallots, chopped
> 1 teaspoon tarragon leaves, chopped
> 1 teaspoon red wine vinegar
> 1 teaspoon tarragon wine vinegar
> 1 tablespoon dry white wine
> 2 egg yolks
> 1 tablespoon hot water
> 1 stick butter clarified (¹/₄ cup)
> ¹/₂ teaspoon lemon juice
> Sea salt
> Pinch of cayenne pepper
> ¹/₂ teaspoon parsley, chopped
> ¹/₂ teaspoon tarragon leaves, chopped

Combine the first 6 ingredients in a small saucepan and cook over medium heat until the liquid evaporates. Be careful not to scorch the reduction. Set aside.

In a copper or stainless steel bowl, whip together with a whisk the 2 egg yolks and 1 tablespoon hot tap water until smooth. Avoid aluminum, as it discolors the yolks.

Cook over very low direct heat or place bowl over a pan of hot, but not boiling, water. Beat continuously, using the whisk to scrape the mixture from the bottom and sides of the bowl. Beating vigorously in a figure-8 pattern incorporates more air, and thereby produces a lighter sauce.

To test for doneness, pull the whisk out of the sauce; a thick ribbon rather than individual streams should form.

Remove from the heat and slowly add the warm clarified butter, whipping constantly. Should sauce begin to separate, add 1 teaspoon cold water.

Whisk in the cooled reduction. Season with lemon juice, salt, and cayenne pepper to taste. Strain the sauce through a fine sieve into a warm—not hot—nonmetallic bowl. Mix in the finely chopped parsley and tarragon leaves.

*Hint:* The egg yolks must be heated gradually over low heat to avoid scrambling them. The sauce must remain at a constant, tepid temperature or it will begin to separate. If the sauce cools, whisk in a teaspoon of warm water. If the sauce curdles from overheating, whisk in 1 teaspoon of cold water.

# Game Marinade

    1 quart olive oil
    8 bay leaves
    12 whole cloves
    ½ teaspoon whole thyme
    ½ teaspoon ground juniper berries
    ½ teaspoon coarse ground pepper
    4 tablespoons finely chopped celery
    1 tablespoon ground garlic
    1 tablespoon finely chopped parsley or herbs

Combine the olive oil, bay leaves, cloves, thyme, juniper, and pepper in a stainless steel saucepan. Place over moderate fire and heat until the oil just begins to boil. Add the remaining ingredients and heat the oil until it just begins to boil a second time. Immediately remove from heat. Allow to cool and store covered in the refrigerator.

# Chive Oil

    ½ cup olive oil
    3 bunches fresh chives
    Sea salt
    Freshly ground pepper

Pick out any wilted or discolored chives and discard.

Finely mince the chives. Combine the minced chives and oil in a food processor. Process for 1-2 minutes until chives are completely puréed. Season with sea salt and pepper to taste.

Place in the refrigerator and allow to mature overnight before using.

# Mayonnaise

Makes $\frac{1}{2}$ cup

> 1 egg yolk
> $\frac{1}{2}$ teaspoon Dijon-style mustard
> $\frac{1}{8}$ teaspoon sea salt
> $\frac{1}{2}$ teaspoon wine vinegar
> Few drops of lemon juice
> $\frac{1}{2}$ cup olive oil
> Freshly ground white pepper

In a stainless steel or ceramic bowl, beat the egg yolk with a wire whisk. Add the mustard, salt, vinegar, and lemon juice, and mix until well blended.

Add the oil by pouring in a slow steady stream and beating continuously. If the sauce becomes too thick, thin it out with $\frac{1}{4}$ teaspoon water.

Add the pepper and taste for seasoning.

# Vinaigrette Dressing

Makes $\frac{1}{2}$ cup

> 1 tablespoon red wine vinegar
> 1 tablespoon balsamic vinegar
> $\frac{1}{2}$ teaspoon finely minced onion
> $\frac{1}{2}$ teaspoon finely minced shallots
> $\frac{1}{2}$ teaspoon finely minced garlic
> $\frac{1}{2}$ teaspoon Dijon-style mustard
> $\frac{1}{2}$ teaspoon dry mustard
> 1 drop Tabasco sauce
> $\frac{1}{2}$ teaspoon chopped fresh tarragon
> Sea salt
> Freshly ground pepper to taste
> $\frac{1}{2}$ cup olive oil

Combine all the ingredients, except the oil, in a small bowl and beat together with a whisk until they are well blended.

Gradually beat in the oil. Taste and adjust seasonings.

*Variation:* Add fresh herbs, such as parsley and chives, to taste. The vinaigrette naturally separates; be sure to shake well before using.

Different brands of mustards, vinegars, and herbs will alter the final product. Adjust according to your preferences.

# Duxelles

1 cup

> 2 tablespoons butter
> ¹/₂ pound finely chopped mushrooms
> 2 tablespoons finely chopped shallots
> ¹/₂ teaspoon lemon juice
> 2 tablespoons heavy whipping cream
> Sea salt
> Freshly ground pepper

Duxelles are cooked chopped mushrooms, a rather thick purée.

In a small saucepan, melt the butter, and add the mushrooms, shallots, and lemon juice.

Cook over high heat until the mushroom moisture evaporates, scrape the bottom of the pan to avoid scorching. Add the heavy cream and season with salt and pepper. Bring to a boil and remove from heat. Refrigerate until ready to use.

# Crêpe Batter

Makes 6 crepes

> 1 large egg
> ¹/₂ cup milk
> 2 teaspoons evaporated cane juice or sugar
> Pinch of sea salt
> 2 rounded tablespoons unbleached flour
> 1¹/₂ tablespoons butter (slightly less than ¹/₂ stick)
> Butter and oil

Break the egg into a mixing bowl and beat thoroughly with a wire whisk. Add the milk, salt, and evaporated cane juice, whisking well.

Add the flour and incorporate completely.

Heat the butter in a small saucepan until the butter is lightly browned and add to the batter while whisking. Allow the batter to rest in the refrigerator for 1 hour before using.

The consistency of the batter is important as the resulting crepes should be very thin. If the batter is too thick and spreads unevenly, add a little more milk. If the batter is too thin, the crepes will have many small holes; add a little more flour.

Use a heavy 6-7 inch iron skillet with sloping sides to fry the crepes. The French use a classic crepe pan which, like their omelet pan, is dedicated to that single use.

Place the crepe pan over high heat and add a small amount of butter and oil, just enough to coat the bottom of the pan. When the butter begins to brown, remove the pan from the heat and ladle about 2 tablespoons of batter into the pan; tilt the pan quickly to evenly coat the bottom with the batter. The crepe should be very thin, so it is important to use only enough batter to coat the bottom of the pan.

Place the pan back over high heat and cook for approximately 1 minute or until nicely browned. Turn with a spatula and fry for another ¹/₂ minute or until brown. Turn the crepe out onto a plate and repeat until the desired number are made.

Allow each crepe to cool before stacking. Crêpes may be prepared ahead and refrigerated before using.

With a little practice you will be able to use several skillets at one time and turn the crepes by flipping the pans and tossing.

# Pastry Syrup

Makes 1½ cups

> ½ cup evaporated cane juice or sugar
> 1 cup water
> 1 tablespoon Kirsch, if desired

THE UTENSILS:

> 1 small saucepan
> 2-4 cups
> Wire whisk

## HOW TO PREPARE:

Combine the evaporated cane juice and water in a small saucepan and boil over high heat. Remove from flame and allow to cool. Stir in the *Kirsch*, if desired. The syrup may be prepared in advance and stored, covered, in the refrigerator.

*Variation:* Just about any liqueur or fruit juice may be mixed with the sugar syrup and used to moisten and flavor the sponge cake.

Fruit and liqueur flavors may be mixed as well as matched.

# Vanilla Custard Sauce

Makes 3 cups

> 1 cup milk
> ½ cup evaporated cane juice or sugar
> ½ teaspoon grated orange rind
> ½ teaspoon lemon rind
> ⅓ vanilla bean split or 2 teaspoons pure vanilla extract
> 3 large egg yolks
> 1 cup heavy whipping cream

THE UTENSILS:

> 1-quart stainless steel or copper saucepan
> 1-quart stainless steel or glass bowl
> Vegetable grater
> Wire whisk
> Rubber spatula or kitchen spoon
> Strainer

Combine the milk, evaporated cane juice, orange and lemon rinds, and split vanilla bean in a heavy copper or stainless steel saucepan. Scald the milk and remove from flame. Strain the milk to remove the vanilla bean and citrus rinds.

Separate the eggs. Reserve the whites for another recipe (they may be frozen). Place the egg yolks in a bowl and whisk thoroughly. Slowly pour the hot milk into the beaten yolks, whisking constantly.

Transfer the mixture back to the saucepan. Cook over very low direct heat, stirring constantly with a spoon or spatula until the custard just begins to boil. Remove from heat and immediately pour in the heavy cream. If you are using vanilla extract, add it at this point. Cool and refrigerate.

*TO SERVE:*

Add Grand Marnier or fruit brandy, 1-2 tablespoons or to taste.

*Hint:* Our method of making custard sauce differs from those of others who caution, "do not boil."

If the mixture separates, whipping at high speed will reconstitute the sauce.

Use the vanilla custard sauce as a base for ice cream. Despite the many high-quality products now available, none equals those freshly made right in your own home.

For chocolate ice cream or chocolate custard sauce, add 3 ounces dark semi-sweet melted chocolate to the above recipe.

# Raspberry-Strawberry Sauce

1 pint fresh raspberries or fresh strawberries
$^1/_3$ cup evaporated cane juice or sugar
1 tablespoon *Framboise*, raspberry brandy, if desired

THE UTENSILS:
Food processor
A fine sieve
Rubber spatula

Clean the berries and place in a food processor with the sweetener. Purée and strain through a fine sieve to remove the seeds. Stir in the brandy, if desired.

*Variation:* Use the same method to prepare Strawberry Sauce. Add *Kirsch* instead of *Framboise*. It is not necessary to strain the strawberry sauce.

# Chocolate Coating

> ¹/₂ cup of heavy whipping cream
> 6 ounces semi-sweet chocolate
> 1 level tablespoon corn syrup

THE UTENSILS:
> 1-quart stainless steel sauce pan
> Wire whisk
> Spatula

Boil the cream in a heavy saucepan, add the chocolate, and stir until the chocolate is completely dissolved. Do not boil again. Add the corn syrup and mix well. Set aside.

*Hint:* Cool the chocolate and store in a tightly covered container. Keep refrigerated. Melt, but do not boil, before using again.


# Hazelnut Paste

THE HAZELNUT BUTTER:
> 1³/₄ cups shelled hazelnuts (approximately ¹/₂ pound)
> 4 tablespoons vegetable oil

*TO PREPARE THE HAZELNUT PASTE:*

*Preheat the oven to 400 degrees.*

Spread the hazelnuts in 1 layer on a sheet pan, and toast in the oven until the skins blister and darken, about 8-10 minutes.

Immediately wrap the hazelnuts in a towel and rub vigorously to remove skins. (Not all of the skins will be removed; however, the outcome will not be affected.) If you are fortunate enough to find blanched hazelnuts, toast 4-5 minutes until lightly browned. Be careful not to over-toast as the hazelnut butter will have a bitter taste.

Place the hazelnuts and oil into a food processor fitted with a steel blade. Process to a coarse paste, approximately 3-4 minutes. Set aside.

# Pastry Cream

Makes 1½ cups

> 1 cup milk
> ¼ vanilla bean (about 1½ inches long) or ¼ teaspoon pure
>     vanilla extract
> Twist each of lemon and orange rind
> 3 large egg yolks
> ⅓ cup plus 1 tablespoon evaporated cane juice or sugar
> 1 tablespoon flour
> 1 tablespoon cornstarch

Combine the milk, vanilla bean, and lemon and orange twists in a copper or stainless steel saucepan. Place over high heat and bring to a boil. Remove vanilla bean and twists.

Beat the egg yolks and ⅓ cup sweetener together in a bowl until the mixture whitens, using a wire whisk or electric mixer. Stir in the flour and cornstarch, blending until smooth.

Slowly pour the hot milk into the egg yolk mixture, beating vigorously with a wire whisk. If you are using vanilla extract instead of vanilla bean, add the extract now.

Pour back into the saucepan, place over medium heat, and boil the mixture for 1 minute, stirring constantly to prevent the custard from sticking to the bottom of the pan.

Pour the pastry cream into a bowl and sprinkle with 1 tablespoon of sweetener. This prevents the formation of skin on the surface. Allow to cool. Cover and refrigerate.

*Variation:* Pastry cream may be flavored in numerous ways. Among our favorites are the *Eaux-de-vie*, fruit brandies, *Kirsch* (cherry), and *Framboise* (raspberry).

# Bibliography

Anchell, Melvin. *The Steak Lovers Diet*. Atlanta: Second Opinion Publishing, 1998.

Calvert, Rita, Nick Lettunich, and Julie Welch. *The Aphrodisiac Cookbook*. Carmel, Calif.: Surfside Publishing, 1980.

Casanova, Giacomo and Willard R. Trask. *History of My Life*. Baltimore: Johns Hopkins University Press, 1997.

Chalmers, Irena. *The Great Food Almanac*. New York: Harper Trade, 1994.

Colbin, Annemarie. *Food & Healing*. New York: Ballantine Publishing Group, 1986.

Diamond, Jared. *Guns, Germs, and Steel*. Scranton: W.W. Norton and Company, 1997.

Douglass, William Campbell. *The Milk Book*. Atlanta: Second Opinion Publishing, 1984.

Dufty, William. *Sugar Blues*. Boston: Warner Books Inc., 1975.

Eramus, Udo. *Fats that Heal, Fats that Kill*. Blaine, Wash.: Alive Books, 1986.

Fallon, Sally. *Nourishing Traditions*. San Diego: ProMotion Publishing, 1995.

Gitteman, Ann Louise, James Templeton, and Candelora Versace. *Your Body Knows Best*. Riverside, N.J.: Pocket Books, 1993.

Gonzales, Nicholas James. "One Man Alone: An Investigation of Nutrition, Cancer and William Donald Kelley." unpublished monograph, 1987.

Hendrickson, Robert. *Lewd Food*. Radnor, Pa.: Chilton Book Company, 1974.

Herbst, Sharon Tyler. *Food Lover's Companion*. Hauppauge, N.Y.: Barron's Educational Series, 1990.

Hopkins, Martha and Randall Lockridge. *Inter Courses*. Waco, Tex.: Terrace Publishing, 1997.

Jensen, Bernard and Mark Anderson. *Empty Harvest*. Garden City Park, N.Y.: Avery Publishing Group Inc., 1990.

Jensen, Bernard. *Foods That Heal*. Garden City Park, N.Y.: Avery Publishing Group Inc., 1988.

Klatz, Ronald. *Grow Young with HGH*. New York: Harper Trade, 1997.

Lang, Jenifer Harvey, ed. *Larousse Gastronomique*. Westminster, Md.: Crown Publishing Group Inc., 1988.

Langre, Jacques de. *Seasalt's Hidden Powers*. Asheville, N.C.: Happiness Press, 1994.

Menzie, Karol V. "Treasured Truffles: Wild Delight," *Baltimore Sun*, 22 Dec. 1999, sec. A La Carte.

Page, Melvin E. and H. Leon Abrams. *Your Body Is Your Best Doctor*. Lincolnwood, Ill.: Keats Publishing Inc., 1972.

Price, Weston A. *Nutrition and Physical Degeneration*. Lincolnwood, Ill.: Keats Publishing, 1945.

Simon Andre L. *A Concise Encyclopedia of Gastronomy*. Woodstock: The Overlook Press, 1952.

Sokolov, Raymond. *Why We Eat What We Eat*. New York: Summit Books, 1991.

Stanley, Kathleen. "The Scoop on Caviar," *Washington Post*, 22 Dec. 1999, sec. Food.

Walker, Morton. *Sexual Nutrition*. Garden City Park, N.Y.: Avery Publishing Group, 1994.

Wolfert, Paula. *The Cooking of South-West France*. Westminster, Md.: Dell Publishing, 1983.

# Index